Allah Loves...

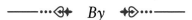 *By*

OMAR SULEIMAN

KUBE
PUBLISHING

In association with

YAQEEN™
INSTITUTE FOR ISLAMIC RESEARCH

Allah Loves...

First published in England by
Kube Publishing Ltd
Markfield Conference Centre
Ratby Lane, Markfield
Leicestershire, LE67 9SY
United Kingdom

Tel: +44 (0) 1530 249230

Website: www.kubepublishing.com
Email: info@kubepublishing.com

Cataloguing-in-Publication Data is available from the
British Library.

ISBN 978-1-84774-135-6 Casebound
ISBN 978-1-84774-136-3 Ebook

Cover design, illustration and typesetting: Jannah Haque
Printed by: IMAK Ofset, Turkey.

Transliteration ⇝ *Guide* ⇜

A brief guide to some of the letters and symbols used in the Arabic transliteration in this book.

th	ث	*ḥ*	ح	*dh*	ذ
ṣ	ص	*ḍ*	ض	*ṭ*	ط
ẓ	ظ	‘	ع	’	ء

ā	ـَا آ	*ī*	ـِي	*ū*	ـُو

ﷺ May the peace and blessings of Allah be upon him.

Contents

Allah Loves...

Introduction

The Prophet Muhammad (*peace be upon him*) said that one of the supplications of Prophet Dāwūd (*peace be upon him*) was that he would say, "اللَّهُمَّ إِنِّي أَسْأَلُكَ حُبَّكَ, O Allah I ask You for Your love, وَحُبَّ مَنْ يُحِبُّكَ, and the love of those who love You, وَالْعَمَلَ الَّذِي يُبَلِّغُنِي حُبَّكَ, and all of the actions that would bring me closer to being loved by You."

Our aim should constantly be to pursue Allah's pleasure; pursue the reward that He has promised. Furthermore, one should avoid the things that He has told us to stay away from, but to *know* that one is loved by Allah, that is the pinnacle. To strive and remain constantly focussed on that goal to pursue Allah's love and to meet Him in that state of love is the most special and sacred level that a human being can attain. In thirty short chapters this book will look at who, and what qualities and characteristics Allah loves and how we may become people who are loved by Allah and do things that Allah loves.

1 Allah Loves
Piety

---•❖•---

The most frequent references in the Qur'an to the love of Allah come in relation to *taqwā*, piety. Surah al-Baqarah starts with this beautiful *āyah*:

الم. ذَلِكَ الْكِتَابُ لاَ رَيْبَ فِيهِ هُدًى لِّلْمُتَّقِينَ

Alif. Lam. Mim. This is a Book in which there is no doubt, it is a guidance for people of taqwā.

People of *taqwā*, people of piety, are the ones Allah loves. He says in the Qur'an: فَإِنَّ اللَّهَ يُحِبُّ الْمُتَّقِينَ,
And Allah loves the people of piety.

The very first command that Allah gives to humanity
in the Qur'an is:

يَا أَيُّهَا النَّاسُ اعْبُدُواْ رَبَّكُمُ الَّذِي خَلَقَكُمْ وَالَّذِينَ مِن قَبْلِكُمْ
لَعَلَّكُمْ تَتَّقُونَ

*O humanity, worship your Lord who created you and
created those who came before you so that you may
have taqwā, so that you may be conscious of Him.*

Specifically, with regards to fasting, Allah declares
to us that:

كُتِبَ عَلَيْكُمُ الصِّيَامُ كَمَا كُتِبَ عَلَى الَّذِينَ مِن قَبْلِكُمْ لَعَلَّكُمْ تَتَّقُونَ
*Fasting was prescribed upon you the way it was
prescribed to those before you so that you may attain
taqwā, so that you may attain piety.*

One may ask how is this connected to Allah's love?

The starting point is how we understand "Divine"
in the first place. Allah created us not to hate us,
but to love us. Allah created us not to fail, but to
succeed. Allah created us not to burn in Hell but
to go to Heaven. He gave us everything that we
needed to attain His reward. He has given us all the
essentials needed to attain His pleasure but do we

clearly understand and comprehend the fact that we are on this path back to Him, that we don't want to do anything that will compromise His love for us?

There is an ongoing debate about what the true meaning of *taqwā* is: does it mean to be in fear of Him, or to be conscious of Him? What does piety even mean? What does it mean to be God-conscious? How can I fear Him if I need to love Him? If you translate for example اَللّٰهُ يُحِبُّ الْمُتَّقِين as *God loves those who fear Him,* then this would need further explanation. Ibn al-Qayyim said that "when you fear something, you run away from it, but when you fear Allah, you run back to Him". And so the fear of Allah is not the kind that would cause you to flee from Him but to come back to Him because that fear is not like the fear of anything else. *Taqwā* is inadequately understood when defined only in a context of fear.

So how do we merge fear and love? We fear losing His love and that is actually why Ramadan is such an effective way for us to learn how to not lose His love. In Ramadan, we observe carefully how and what we consume. We physically make sure that we don't consume anything that is going to nullify our fast. Likewise, in our daily lives we make sure that we don't consume anything that would spiritually nullify Allah's love for us. We pay closer attention to ourselves. The narration that really encapsulates this is that from ʿUmar (*may Allah be pleased with him*) who said that, "*Taqwā* is like a person who's walking on a path again and again, and on this path back to Allah there are thorny bushes on the way, when they witness these thorny bushes close to them, they pull themselves in tighter to make sure that the thorns don't tear their clothes or prick them." And ʿUmar's grandson, ʿUmar ibn ʿAbd al-ʿAzīz, said that "*Taqwā* isn't praying long into the night, it isn't fasting long into the day; it is that you abandon everything that is displeasing to Allah. Everything beyond that is *iḥsān*, is excellence."

Tying *taqwā* to the love of Allah is very important. Are we showing Allah that we want to be loved by Him? Are we demonstrating it by our deeds in a translatable way, that we're not going to do anything that is going to dissatisfy His pleasure? Imam al-Ghazālī said something very profound, "The greatest consequence of sin is not the punishment that comes with it, but the distance that comes between you and Allah." If we were created by God to return to Him in a state that is pleasing to Him and if He has given us everything that is needed to do so, then to demonstrate our desire to be loved, we should show caution with things that compromise that love. *Taqwā* is that constant effort and mindset that we are steering back to Allah, and the most practical way to deal with this is, that when we're thinking about saying something that is displeasing to Allah, we stop ourselves because we don't want to earn His displeasure. When we see something, and we don't stare at it because we know it could earn the displeasure of Allah. When we're about to do something that could earn the displeasure of Allah, we stop ourselves because we know that the greatest consequence is distance from Him. Indeed, the greatest way to be loved by Allah is to show we fear losing that love.

May Allah allow us to never compromise our love for Him, and may Allah entrench within us *taqwā*, that God-consciousness, and may Allah keep us in His favour. *Āmīn*.

Indeed, the greatest way to be loved by Allah is to show we fear losing that love.

2 Allah Loves
Repentance

As discussed in the previous chapter, with *taqwā* or piety, we have to avoid the thorny bushes that are on the road to Allah. We are meant to go back to Allah, but these obstacles keep getting in the way. We are inevitably going to be pricked by a thorn and there's absolutely nothing we can do about it. The Prophet (*peace be upon him*) said, "Every single one of the children of Adam is a sinner." Every single one of us is going to commit sins, is going to get pricked. We're going to fall behind and the best amongst us are those who are going to come back to Allah, وَخَيْرُ الْخَطَّائِينَ التَّوَّابُونَ, *the best of those who make mistakes are the ones who repent to Allah.*

This is very important to understand, after going through the concept of *taqwā* and not committing sins, Allah mentions that اَللّٰهُ يُحِبُّ التَّوَّابِينَ, *Allah loves those who repent,* again framed within the love of Allah.

Allah didn't create us to not sin. Allah created us to know how to deal with sin properly and there is a major difference between the two. The word *tawbah* means turning back to Allah, not necessarily that we have removed all the effects of that sin. Realize that even the word "repentance" relates to our relationship with Allah.

So, how does that work? Being sinful is part of our humanity, and forgiveness is part of Allah's attributes. If we pair those two together, then we acknowledge our sinfulness even when we intentionally committed a sin. We acknowledge our sin and we try to get back on the path to Allah. In doing so, we actually raise our degree of favour with Allah, because He loves *al-tawwābīn*, the penitent, those who turn back to Him. The Prophet (*peace be upon him*) mentions that "If you were not to sin

8

There is no such thing as a sin that can permanently disqualify you from the love of Allah if you repent afterwards and use that to propel yourself towards Him.

then Allah would have replaced you with a people who would. Then they would seek forgiveness and would be forgiven by Allah, because He loves to forgive. Allah loves repentance and He loves those who repent." It is beautiful, that in pairing sin and forgiveness together, in Islam there is no such thing as failure—unless you don't do anything about that failure. There is no such thing as a sin that can permanently disqualify you from the love of Allah if you repent afterwards and use that to propel yourself towards Him. What the Prophet (*peace be upon him*) is teaching us here is the effect of seeking forgiveness on the heart. The Prophet (*peace be upon him*) said that the dark spot placed in the heart by sin is polished, not just removed, by repentance. As for the effect of repentance on our deeds the Prophet (*peace be upon him*) said, "The sin is actually turned into a good deed on your scrolls." Upon true repentance, that bad deed actually becomes a good deed, a *ḥasanah*.

As for the effect of repentance on us with regards to Allah's love: إِنَّ اللهَ يُحِبُّ التَّوَّابِينَ, *Allah loves the penitent,* those who always turn back towards Him.

Repentance means we actually get closer to Allah than we were before we committed the sin, we become more beloved to Him than before. This is why it's not unjust that Allah created us and gave us the free will to sin, because the degree that He guarantees us for repenting after committing a sin is even greater than that of His sinless creatures, the angels, who have no free will. Penitent human beings ascend even beyond the angels in rank.

Ibn al-Qayyim puts the ideas together and gives us the examples of two Prophets. He explained that *Shayṭān*, the Devil, was delighted when he saw that he had caused Adam's fall. What he didn't realize was that when a diver goes into the ocean, he collects pearls at the bottom, and he rises back up again. Adam was better after his *tawbah* even though he had to come down to this earth. His rank with Allah was higher after his repentance than when he was in Paradise. In the same way Yūnus or Jonas was better after he was swallowed by the whale than he was before it happened. That's why Allah says: فَاجْتَبَاهُ رَبُّهُ فَجَعَلَهُ مِنَ الصَّالِحِينَ, *His Lord chose him and made him from the righteous,* after he was swallowed by the whale. After Yūnus had prayed to Allah: لَّا إِلَـٰهَ إِلَّا أَنتَ سُبْحَانَكَ إِنِّي كُنتُ مِنَ الظَّالِمِينَ, *There is no god but You, how perfect You are and I was amongst the wrong-doers.* So again our hearts are polished, our sins are turned into good deeds and our ranks ascend in the sight of Allah after we turn back to Him.

We have a Lord that created our past, present, and future. It doesn't matter what we did in the past because He guaranteed us a better future if we learn how to deal with that past, and that will propel us towards Him. We ask Allah to make us amongst those that are beloved to Him in our repentance and in our sin, and in our good deeds. *Āmīn.*

3 Allah Loves
Excellence

The most praiseworthy station in the sight of Allah, the highest quality that was manifested in the Prophet (*peace be upon him*) was the quality of *iḥsān*, the quality of excellence. *Taqwā* is the stepping stone to *iḥsān*. God-consciousness is the stepping stone towards excellence.

The Prophet (*peace be upon him*) described *iḥsān* as "worshipping Allah as if you can see Him, and if you can't see Him, then know that He sees you". If we remember the statement of ʿUmar ibn ʿAbd al-ʿAzīz in the first chapter, he defined *taqwā* as a person abandoning sins, and everything beyond that—like fasting long into the day or praying long into the night—are forms of excellence or *iḥsān.*

So how do these qualities work together? *Taqwā* is remembering that Allah sees everything so that we are deterred from doing anything that could compromise His love. *Iḥsān* is honouring the sight of Allah upon us in a way that would encourage us to earn extra love from Allah. It beautifies our obligatory deeds and then it leads us to do deeds that aren't expected of us, to hold ourselves to higher standards because we don't want to be just another average person. We don't want to just love Allah: we want to be "in love" with Allah. We don't just want to get by with obligatory good deeds, but want to do more and more till we distinguish ourselves and become among those who are especially loved by Allah.

Allah mentions throughout the Qur'an وَاللّٰهُ يُحِبُّ الْمُحْسِنِينَ, *and Allah loves those who do good (al-muḥsinīn),* almost in exact proportion to the mention of Allah's love of *taqwā. Iḥsān* is described in the Qur'an and the Sunnah of the Prophet (*peace be upon him*) both as how we interact with Allah and also how we interact with people. With regards to Allah, we go beyond the obligatory and do that which is voluntary. We don't look at people around us, or whether other people are looking at us or not. We are always focused on only the sight of Allah upon us, and that shows itself in the way that we rise above social approval and the way that we beautify our deeds.

To explain the way that it manifests itself in our relationship with people, Allah talks about *iḥsān* in a variety of situations that we actually find ourselves in, الَّذِينَ يُنْفِقُونَ فِي السَّرَّاءِ وَالضَّرَّاءِ, *those who spend both in times of ease and in times of hardship.* When a person is at ease, they give more than the required amount of zakat, beyond that which is obligatory. They open their hands and hearts and keep on giving charity. And when they are in hardship—just like they wouldn't want Allah to stop providing for them, even if they were distant or even if they were doing things that should disqualify them from sustenance—they too continue to give even when no one expects it of them, even when they are in hardship, because they understand that Allah is the Provider and the One worth spending for and no person goes into poverty for giving towards Allah.

They measure themselves by different standards: they spend in ease, and they spend in hardship, وَالْكَاظِمِينَ الْغَيْظ, *and they swallow their anger even when their anger is justified.* They don't just avoid doing the things that are haram in anger, but they also make sure that they swallow their anger so that it is used only for good. They don't use their anger for things that are petty. They don't use their anger for things that are displeasing to Allah. They control their anger even when it may be justified because they want Allah to withhold His anger from them. وَالْعَافِينَ عَنِ النَّاسِ, *And they pardon people* even when they are in the right.

Islam establishes the right of a person to take back what's been wrongly taken from them, to fulfil their sense of justice. Justice is the societal standard but when it comes to achieving personal excellence, once justice has been afforded, they opt to forgive and to show mercy and to pardon, because that's what they seek from Allah, that is *iḥsān*.

Allah says: أَلَا تُحِبُّونَ أَن يَغْفِرَ اللهُ لَكُمْ, ***Don't you want Allah to pardon you and to forgive you?*** Even when you find yourself undeserving? The way to describe *iḥsān* is that you see the love of Allah through all your interactions and you aim for a higher degree of the love of Allah through your interactions. You hold yourself to a higher standard, whether it's in your worship, your relationships, your work ethics—and you are doing this because the degree of Allah's love that you seek is that much higher.

Allah describes three types of selves in the Qur'an: the first إِنَّ النَّفْسَ لَأَمَّارَةٌ بِالسُّوءِ, ***the soul that commands itself with evil,*** that indulges in evil. The second, ***the soul that is accountable,*** النَّفْسُ اللَّوَّامَةُ, that's the self of *taqwā*, of holding yourself accountable, of trying not to do anything that disqualifies you from the love of Allah. And the third: النَّفْسُ المُطْمَئِنَّةُ, ***the soul that is at peace*** with Allah, that is the self of *iḥsān*, that's the person of excellence, because they are at peace with the favour of their Lord, and they always pursue their Lord's favour even in the most unfavourable situations in life.

We ask Allah to make us from the *muhsinīn*, who are at peace with the favour of their lord, who will always find His excellent favour on the Day of Judgment, and to be amongst those motivated by His love before anything else. *Āmīn.*

4 Allah Loves
Angelic Praise

Iḥsān or excellence allows us to pursue a higher degree of Allah's love. It is what makes us a special human being because we're choosing to worship Allah at a higher level. This is precisely what Imam Ḥasan al-Baṣrī (*Allah's mercy be upon him*) meant when he said that Allah allows a human being to be elevated in His Sight, to a rank even above that of an angel. It is because an angel has no choice but to obey Allah whereas a human being goes beyond obedience, carrying out acts of voluntary praise, voluntary love, and voluntary worship. They distinguish themselves in the sight of Allah and are elevated to a higher position in Paradise as a result.

The Prophet (*peace be upon him*) told a Companion of his who was glorifying Allah with words of praise, "Increase in praise because الْحَمْدَ يُحِبُّ رَبَّكَ إِنَّ, your Lord loves to be praised." In another narration, the Prophet (*peace be upon him*) was asked by Abu Dharr (*May Allah's mercy be upon him*), "what are the words that are most beloved to Allah?", the Prophet (*peace be upon him*) said "وبِحَمْدِهِ اللهِ سُبْحَانَ, My Lord is glorified, my Lord is perfect and may He be praised."

When we say اللهِ سُبْحَانَ, we are praising the perfection of Allah. When we say لله اَلْحَمْدُ we are praising Him in that perfection and adding into that *thanā'* and *shukr*, the element of praise and gratitude, so *subḥān Allāhi wa bi-ḥamdihī* really adds to that gratitude, both the declaration of Allah's perfection and of our imperfection, and then the declaration of gratitude and praise in light of Allah's perfection and our own imperfection.

Although the third Hadith has the same words, it gives a very beautiful message and meaning. Abu Dharr narrates that the Prophet (*peace be upon him*) was asked, "What are the most beloved words of praise in the sight of Allah?" The Prophet (*peace be upon him*) replied, الَّذِي اصْطَفَاهُ لِمَلَائِكَتِهِ "The words that Allah chose for His angels", سُبْحَانَ اللهِ وِبَحَمْدِهِ، سُبْحَانَ اللهِ الْعَظِيمِ "How perfect is my Lord and may He be praised, how perfect is my Lord, the Almighty" So the Prophet (*peace be upon him*) said, "These were the words that Allah chose for the angels to glorify Him with", and that is the reason why they are the most beloved of words.

When we rise beyond the angels, when we choose to glorify Him with those words in a heartfelt way and in a way that manifests itself in our actions and in the pursuit of Allah's love, that is when we will start to begin achieving a notable status.

The Prophet (*peace be upon him*) said, كَلِمَتَانِ حَبِيبَتَانِ إِلَى الرَّحْمَنِ, these are the two expressions that are the most beloved to the Most Merciful, خَفِيفَتَانِ عَلَى اللِّسَانِ ثَقِيلَتَانِ فِي الْمِيزَانِ، سُبْحَانَ اللهِ وِبَحَمْدِهِ، سُبْحَانَ اللهِ الْعَظِيمِ they are light on the tongue, but these two expressions are the heaviest on the Scales (*al-mīzān*). They are

21

'How perfect is my Lord and may He be praised, how perfect is my Lord, the Almighty'." This is the expression that matches the *iḥsān* (excellence) in pursuit. We should aim to always keep our tongue busy with these two expressions that are most beloved to the Most Merciful; to continue to praise Allah with them.

We ask Allah to make us amongst those that become praiseworthy by our praise of Him, we ask Allah to make us amongst those who try to pursue that praise in trying to perfect ourselves in understanding His own perfection. *Āmīn.*

5 Allah Loves
Sincere Supplication

In the previous chapter we talked about how Allah loves to be praised. Allah doesn't just love to be praised, He loves to hear our voice. Even asking of Him (*du'ā'*) is generally broken down into *"al-thanā' wa'l-ṭalab"*, which is to praise Him and then to ask Him.

Just to take an example of a person. If we're dealing with someone who is unwilling, incapable or stingy, and if we ask them too much, usually they will stop liking us, maybe even stop loving us. We might love someone as a person, but if they keep on calling us and asking us for things, that

usually turns us off; we may even stop talking to
them or answering their calls because we know
that they're going to keep on asking for things from
us. But, with Allah, not only does our praising
Him bring us closer, but our asking of Him, brings
us closer to Him. This really is such an incredible
concept that sets the Divine apart from us.

The Prophet (*peace be upon him*) said, as was
mentioned in the last chapter, إِنَّ رَبَّكَ يُحِبُّ الْحَمْدَ
that your lord loves to be praised. In another
Hadith in al-Tirmidhī, the Prophet (*peace be upon
him*) mentioned سَلُوا اللهَ مِنْ فَضْلِهِ ؛ فَإِنَّ اللهَ يُحِبُّ أَنْ يُسْأَلَ,
ask Allah from His bounty because Allah loves to
be asked. And the Prophet (*peace be upon him*) said
وإِنَّ أَفْضَلَ العِبَادَةِ انْتِظَارُ الفَرَج, that the best form of
worship is waiting for relief to come from Allah.

In Surah al-Baqarah Allah mentions that He loves
to be called upon through sincere supplication:
وَإِذَا سَأَلَكَ عِبَادِي عَنِّي فَإِنِّي قَرِيبٌ أُجِيبُ دَعْوَةَ الدَّاعِ إِذَا دَعَانِ
that **when My servants ask of Me I am near, I answer
the call of the caller when he calls upon Me.** This
verse is usually given to us in the context of

understanding that Allah is close to us and Allah will answer us. However, if this verse were cut short and it just said: وَإِذَا سَأَلَكَ عِبَادِي عَنِّي فَإِنِّي قَرِيبٌ, *When my servants ask of Me I am near,* that nearness (*qurb*) of Allah is in itself, the biggest blessing that comes from our *du'ā'*. Allah gives a direct response and says فَإِنِّي قَرِيبٌ, *that I am close to you* and that's the biggest gift that can be given to us as a result of calling upon Him.

Therefore, how Allah answers that *du'ā'* is secondary to the fact that we have a direct connection with Him and we have a Lord that loves to hear our voice. Allah is shy from the hands of His servants, and loves to hear the voice of His servant. 'Umar (*Allah's mercy be upon him*) said that إِنِّي لَا أَحْمِلُ هَمَّ الإِجَابَةِ وَلَكِنْ أَحْمِلُ هَمَّ الدُّعَاءِ, "When I make *du'ā'*, I don't concern myself with the response; the only thing that I concern myself with is the ability to make the supplication (*hamm al-du'ā'*)."

If Allah allows us to make supplication then know that we are in a good place, that we are in a relationship with Allah. So, the ability to call upon Him, knowing that Allah loves to hear me,

The ability to
call upon Allah,
knowing that
He loves to hear
me, despite how
broken and sinful
I am, in that there
is a blessing.

despite how broken I am, despite how sinful I am, despite how distant I am with Allah, yet He loves to hear me—in that there is a blessing.

There is a beautiful saying from Ibn ʿAṭāʾillāh (*may Allah be pleased with him*),

مَتَى أَطْلَقَ اللهُ لِسَانَكَ بِالطَّلَبِ فَاعْلَمْ أَنَّهُ يُرِيدُ أَنْ يُعْطِيَكَ

that anytime Allah unshackles your tongue to allow it to ask, any time He allows your tongue to move, any time Allah allows you to make a request, know that Allah wants to give you something because He wouldn't have allowed you to make that *duʿāʾ* unless He wanted to answer that *duʿāʾ* and the greatest gift of that *duʿāʾ* is that Allah loves to hear it and you get closer to Him as a result of it.

وَإِذَا سَأَلَكَ عِبَادِي عَنِّي فَإِنِّي قَرِيبٌ أُجِيبُ دَعْوَةَ الدَّاعِ إِذَا دَعَانِ

When My servants ask you about Me, tell them I am quite near. I hear and answer the call of the caller whenever he calls Me. So when we call upon Allah, He is close to us—that's the first gift. The second gift is that He answers our call in a way that befits us, in a way that's in our best interests, in a way that is beneficial to our worldly life and Hereafter and that doesn't put us in a more detrimental situation because of our limited scope, فَلْيَسْتَجِيبُوا لِي وَلْيُؤْمِنُوا بِي لَعَلَّهُمْ يَرْشُدُونَ, *let them answer Me, let them believe in Me so that they may find guidance* in their life, in both their worldly actions but more importantly in their religious affairs. The Prophet (*peace be upon him*) said سَلِ اللهَ مِنْ فَضْلِهِ, "Ask Allah from His bounty because you have a Lord that loves to be asked."

May Allah make us amongst those whose tongues and whose hearts are always connected to Him, both in praise and in request. *Āmīn.*

6 Allah Loves
Those Who
Are Trying

Most people don't call out to Allah sincerely because they feel too distant from Him to do so. They don't realize that calling out to Him is a way of closing that gap and actually reducing that distance.

Shayṭān invites us to commit sin in the first place, this causes distance between us and Allah, then *Shayṭān* invites us to feel too ashamed to turn back to Allah with *tawbah,* and to call upon Him with *duʿā*'s so that we can get close to Him. This is a very powerful connection that Allah makes in Surah al-Baqarah

إِنَّ اللهَ يُحِبُّ التَّوَّابِينَ وَيُحِبُّ الْمُتَطَهِّرِينَ, *Allah loves those who repent and He loves those who engage in purifying themselves.*

Some scholars interpreted this *āyah* to mean physical purification such as *wuḍū'* and *ṭahārah*: it is referring to the way we clean ourselves up for prayer.

There are other scholars that say that this has a spiritual implication. I want to focus on this from a spiritual perspective. Allah loves *al-mutaṭahhirīn,* or those engaged in purifying themselves, just as He loves those engaged in repentance, not necessarily those, who repented in the past tense because they are no longer committing sin, but who are seeking to purify themselves, who are engaged in the act of purification. Allah does not expect us to reach the peak of purification before we can be worthy of supplicating, Allah loves us just for trying. He loves us just for the effort and if we think about how beautiful and profound that is, then it helps us to repent and make *du'ā'*.

There is a very beautiful explanation for this verse, from a spiritual perspective by Imam Ḥasan al-Baṣrī, as well as from the great explainer (*mufassir*) of the Qur'an Mujāhid (*Allah's mercy be upon him*), who said that إِنَّ اللهَ يُحِبُّ التَّوَّابِينَ, *Allah loves those who repent,* i.e. those who don't insist upon sin and don't return to the same sin. They said وَلَمْ يُصِيبُوهَا, those who don't engage in or those who don't insist upon committing those particular sins, so they're insisting on returning to Allah. Even if they do commit those sins at times; they insist upon returning to Allah. And the second explanation they gave was, وَالْمُتَطَهِّرِينَ لَا يَعُودُونَ إِلَيْهَا, they don't repeat the same sins over and over again as that would show disregard of Allah, that would show that they weren't taking their repentance (*tawbah*) seriously, and that would show that they hadn't learnt this lesson.

There is something important to understand here, Allah loves us for trying, for being engaged in a state of purification. Allah loves us for repenting but where is it that we fall short? Those of us who repent sincerely for a sin and insist we will not return to that sin, yet still do so, that doesn't disqualify us from the love of Allah nor does it open up all the previous times we committed that sin nor does it nullify our previous repentance for that sin. But the type of insistence and returning to sin that could cause us to fall out of the love of Allah, out of this journey of attaining His love, is when we insist upon those sins and disregard the sight of Allah, and disregard the pursuit of Allah by returning to those sins. So there's a difference between falling short again, becoming weak again after we sincerely repent and not being sincere in our repentance or in our pursuit of purification in the first place.

We ask Allah to allow us to always be engaged in the effort of purification, to allow us to reach better states, and to always allow us to be in the state of His love even as we fall short, being in the state of repentance and being in the state of making effort for our purification. *Āmīn.*

7 Allah Loves

⇥ *Tears* ⇤
and Traces

───────── ⬥ ─────────

T he Prophet (*peace be upon him*) said that, "There are no two drops more beloved to Allah than a tear that is shed in awe of Allah and a drop of blood that is shed in a noble struggle for Allah." Then he added that "There are no traces more beloved to Allah than the trace left on a person in the cause of Allah, in the noble struggle for Allah's sake, in the course of carrying out an obligation for Allah's pleasure, or in worshipping Allah." Now obviously this Hadith should first be understood through the lives of the Companions of the Prophet (*peace be upon him*).

If we lived with the Prophet (*peace be upon him*)
then we would have gone through various battles,
if we weren't killed in Badr, Uhud or Khandaq or
any of these battles, then we would probably had
been wounded, had a limp through injury, or some
other mark left on us. The Companions would see
someone with a limp or injury and the Prophet
(*peace be upon him*) would say that this person will
not have that limp or injury in Paradise. This was
comforting to the people who were physically being
wounded because they were Muslims and suffering
for the cause and sake of Allah.

The Prophet (*peace be upon him*) said that on the
Day of Judgement a person would be asked
عَنْ جَسَدِهِ فِيمَا أَبْلَاهُ, about their bodies and what they
did with them. So here the significance of tears is
obvious. Tears engage us in a more spiritual and
deeper form of connection with Allah—in our
supplication, our worship, our repentance; and
what is specifically meant here is in the capacity of
repentance and acknowledging the awesomeness of
Allah as we remember Him. The Prophet (*peace be
upon him*) mentioned that the eye that sheds a tear

The Prophet ﷺ mentioned that the eye that sheds a tear for Allah would not be touched by the fire.

for Allah wouldn't be touched by fire: it wouldn't face any type of punishment from Allah out of the virtue of shedding that tear.

Furthermore, brokenness has actual effects on our body. If any of us have been to *ḥajj*, and may Allah allow all of us the blessing of a sincere and accepted *ḥajj*, we see the pilgrims on the Day of ʿArafah in their pilgrim's garb of *iḥrām*. They haven't slept for days, have dust on their faces, and bags under their eyes because of sleep deprivation. They look so exhausted and tired: no one looks their best on the Plain of ʿArafāt. The Prophet (*peace be upon him*) mentioned that Allah loves to boast to the angels on the Day of ʿArafah and says, "Look at all these servants of Mine that have come to Me from all over the world, their hair unkept, their faces dusty, deprived of rest, and all they ask for is My mercy and My favour." The Prophet (*peace be upon him*) and his Companions went through that. They went through days and nights of struggle for Allah. The Prophet (*peace be upon him*) mentioned a person whose hair becomes grey in a state of Islam, a person who incurs some sort of injury in the cause of Allah.

All these things are significant, and Allah sees them, as traces of evidence that a servant of Allah went through struggle for Him.

The grandson of the Prophet (*peace be upon him*), Zayn al-ʿĀbidīn. When he passed away, he had marks on his back from the bags he used to carry for charity. When Allah talks about the marks of prostration (*athar al-sujūd*), this means more than just a physical mark. It is something that enlightens the faces of the servants of Allah. You notice some people who have a physical mark of *sujūd* on their foreheads from all the years that they spent prostrating to Allah.

All these signs portray brokenness. Clearly, we're not taught to hurt ourselves: I'm not telling anyone to cut themselves, shed blood and then say this is for the sake of Allah. But think about all those times Allah saw you struggling to pray. Maybe you had an injury and praying became harder for you. Those elderly people who pray for the sake of Allah. They shed tears of brokenness and vulnerability. The body shows signs of wear and tear but if it's for something that is good, Allah sees that and knows that we're doing that for Him. We ask Allah to allow us to cry sincerely for His sake, not in a way that makes us feel hopeless but rather hopeful that the One Who sees our tears, our prayers doesn't let them go in vain.

May Allah heal our brokenness, may Allah see us in our weakness and make it a reason for strength, and may Allah bind us closer to Him through those moments when we feel distant from Him. May Allah allow us to be used and consumed in ways that are good and in ways that are pleasing to Him. *Āmīn.*

8 Allah Loves

→ *Trust* ←

One thing that causes people to become disillusioned in their journey towards Allah is when they stop trusting in Him, when they start feeling that things in their lives are out of control, even though they did their *du'ā'*, they did their *tawbah*. They might think to themselves, "I supplicated, I repented, I sought closeness to Allah but things aren't going right". And because they aren't going right they start to question the substance of their *du'ā'*, whether their *tawbah* was accepted, whether their repentance was accepted and all of that serves as a major hindrance between them and Allah.

Ibn 'Abbas, the cousin of Prophet (*peace be upon him*), said that whoever establishes their belief in the Divine decree—truly has a sense of *qadar,* an understanding that Allah is always in charge—establishes their monotheism (*tawhīd*); but whoever lacks this belief, then their entire premise for accepting a Creator, their entire premise for monotheism, is going to be shaky and faulty. So it's important for us to solidify our belief in the Divine decree, as much as we can, and focus upon reliance on Allah (*tawakkul*) in the context of loving Him.

Firstly, Allah mentions إِنَّ اللهَ يُحِبُّ الْمُتَوَكِّلِينَ that *Allah loves those who put their trust in Him.* Why does Allah love those who rely on Him? What are the implications of that and what does that station look like? Firstly, it's in the capacity of إِنَّ اللهَ يُحِبُّ أَنْ يُسْأَلَ, *Allah loves to be asked.* So putting our trust in Him means that we are expressing our love for Him and we are expressing our desire to be nourished and sustained by Him. We make *du'ā',* we ask of Him because we put our trust in Him, acknowledging His power, acknowledging His attributes. Allah loves that we put our trust in Him.

Secondly, Allah removes distractions from Him in this process of trust. If we are constantly feeling like things are out of control and that we have to get everything right while everything is falling apart, then naturally we are going to feel disturbed because things aren't going the way we feel they should. We will not be able to focus our attention on Allah because we are distracted and disturbed by all that is happening around us. That doesn't mean that we should be lazy: just say that I love Allah and I have trust. Rather as things are unfolding in our life around us, we try to maintain perspective and see Allah through all of that and put our trust in Him.

Thirdly, is the station of being a *mutawakkil,* the station of being someone who has that trust of Allah and longing for reward in the Hereafter. If we think that God is punishing us in this life and that we are living in perpetual punishment then it's very hard for us to believe in a place of perpetual reward. *Tawakkul* here allows us to have tranquillity in this life and a sense of longing for the Hereafter.

Allah loves to be asked. So putting our trust in Him means that we are expressing our love for Him and we are expressing our desire to be nourished and sustained by Him.

Ibn Qayyim al-Jawziyyah (*may Allah have mercy on him*) summarizes this very beautifully, in observing that there are three ways or levels to trust Allah. He says the first level of trust in Allah is the way that we would trust an agent (*wakīl*). When we trust an agent then the agent is still in service to us, we are not in service to the agent. We give the agent instructions and when the agent doesn't do exactly what we tell him or her to do, we lose trust in that agent and we try to replace them. Allah isn't going to be this type of *wakīl* for us, we have to move it up.

The second level of trust is the type that a child has for their mother. A child goes to their mother knowing that no one loves them more than her and no one offers them a greater sense of comfort; so even if she punishes the child and it cries and has a tantrum, it still goes back to its mother for comfort because the child trusts its mother's love and knows she has their best interests at heart even when she punishes her child.

He explained the third level of trust in Allah as being like the trust a dead person being washed has on those washing him. That is an absolute state of trust in Allah, complete trust that He will not move us in a direction out of hatred or one that is not in our best interest, complete trust that He will maintain our affairs, that He will see us through every difficulty and that every difficulty is meant for us to gain a further perspective and further closeness to Him on that path to His love. So that highest level of trust in our relationship with Allah allows us to focus on His love for us. Where there is mistrust, there can't be true love.

As Allah mentions إِنَّ اللهَ يُحِبُّ الْمُتَوَكِّلِينَ, *Allah loves those who trust Him.* We ask Allah to make us amongst them. *Āmīn.*

⑨ Allah Loves
Patience

───────── ···✦··· ─────────

Allah mentions in the Qur'an وَاللّٰهُ يُحِبُّ الصَّابِرِينَ *Allah loves those who are patient.* He loves those people who are engaged in patience. The connection of patience to trust is obvious, we can't be patient with Allah if we don't trust Him. We can't be patient with how things are going in life until we understand that there is someone who has control of our life. We are not going to be able to restrain ourselves from acting out unless we have a solid understanding that Allah is acting in a way that is in our best favour. This connection between *ṣabr* and *tawakkul* is necessary and Allah mentions that He loves those who trust Him and loves those who are patient.

Asking Allah to make us a patient person is a good thing, asking Allah for the quality of *ṣabr* that makes us amongst those who are patient is a good thing. However, patience is not just restricted to hard times: patience is something that we practice throughout our lives with Allah. How do we do so? Patience in hardship is obvious. We earn Allah's love when we are patient in hardship because we choose to restrain ourselves for His reward and for His pleasure instead.

'Abdullāh ibn Masʿūd (*Allah's mercy be upon him*) said something very profound in this regard, "Most people on the Day of Judgment don't enter Jannah because of some good deeds that they did but because of the hardship that they faced and the patience that they showed in response to it." So we prepare our whole life and a major trial is thrust upon us, but we express our patience with Allah, our love of Allah despite that hardship, purely based upon the foundation of trust (*tawakkul*) and that allows us to attain the ultimate reward from Allah. To receive Allah's pleasure on the Day of Judgement for our patience in hardship is tremendous, therefore, we hold ourselves back and practise restraint because we see His pleasure rather than our own misfortunes, we see Allah's goal for us rather than our immediate hardship. That goal is able to see us through the imminent hardship, for with patience comes ease.

Patience with regards to our own desires (*shahwah*) is another great virtue. We hold ourselves back from acting upon our lusts and our desires in ways that are impermissible. That's why Allah calls fasting (*sawm*) patience and says وَاسْتَعِينُوا بِالصَّبْرِ وَالصَّلَاةِ, *seek closeness through patience and prayer.* What the scholars say is that the word "patience" is actually replacing the word "fasting" here.

The act that we should also be engaged in, is restraining ourselves in times of ease. When people lose patience in times of ease, they act upon those desires as quickly as they can because they think that they only live once. But that is not true, we know that our life is eternal, our days may be numbered in this world but the Hereafter is for eternity. So why do we rush to act upon those desires and to live out all of our lusts and try to consume all the blessings that are around us or all the trials disguised as blessings around us because we think we are not going to live again after this?

To be patient in our ease and patient with our desires by restraining ourselves because we know that the reward Allah guaranteed us in the Hereafter is far greater than anything that we could have in this life. The element of Allah's pleasure and reward is able to get us through our ease just as it is able to get us through hardship.

The last form of patience that the scholars have mentioned is the patience in our worship with Allah. If we are not patient in worshipping Allah and upholding the commands of Allah upon us then that shows a lack of regard for Allah. Patience in the maintenance of those acts of worship are a form of expression that we are willing to stay the course for the sake of Allah because we want to see these good deeds accepted, done correctly and done with *iḥsān*, in a way that shows excellence and in return for that وَاللّٰهُ يُحِبُّ الصَّابِرِينَ, *and Allah loves the patient.* May Allah make us amongst them. *Āmīn.*

⑩ Allah Loves
Justice

·····❖·····

As was mentioned earlier, the two most common occurrences of *Allah loves* in the Qur'an are إِنَّ اللهَ يُحِبُّ الْمُتَّقِين and إِنَّ اللهَ يُحِبُّ الْمُحْسِنِينَ, *Allah loves those who observe piety* and *Allah loves those who observe excellence.* The third most common occurrence in the Qur'an is إِنَّ اللهَ يُحِبُّ الْمُقْسِطِينَ, *Allah loves those who are just;* Allah loves those who are equitable.

When we think about justice, we often think about the big picture; we think about a ruler, an authority, a government. We think about all of these huge systems that exist outside of our immediate control. But

consider that the references to justice in the Qur'an
are usually talking about things that we actually
encounter on a daily basis. Allah talks about how He
hates oppression, how He hates transgression, Allah
hates all of the things that demonstrate inequity. But
when it comes to us in our individual lives, Allah
praises those who do justice and those who are
equitable. Allah says He loves those who are just.
وَلاَ يَجْرِمَنَّكُمْ شَنَآنُ قَوْمٍ عَلَى أَلاَّ تَعْدِلُواْ, *don't let the hatred of
a people cause you to be unjust with them.* He loves
those people that are just even with the people that
they don't like and that earns them the love of Allah.
Allah says إِنَّ اللهَ يُحِبُّ الْمُقْسِطِينَ, in Surah al-Ḥujurāt
where He talks about a person who brings two sides
or groups, that are in disagreement or suffering in-
fighting, together. This is something that could be
happening in our family, in our workplace or our
community; in situations where we can play the role
of *iṣlāḥ*, rectifying the situation, reconciling between
the parties but most importantly maintaining a sense
of justice.

The scholars warned us not to read traditions about
the just ruler, who is the first person shaded by Allah

Allah loves those who are just and hates those who oppress and oppression is a disqualification from the love of Allah.

under His Throne on the Day of Judgement, or the one who is given a pulpit of light just in the context of the sultan, the imam, ruler, government or authority. But rather we should see ourselves as capable of attaining these positions. Every single one of us is placed in a situation, sometimes in multiple situations, sometimes even on a daily basis, where we have the ability to either be a vehicle of justice in someone else's life or to uphold it in our own immediate lives with the things that are around us.

إِنَّ اللهَ يُحِبُّ الْمُقْسِطِينَ, *Allah loves those who are just* and hates those who oppress and oppression is a disqualification from the love of Allah. Each one of us should look at our lives and ask, "If I'm being unjust now, then how will that fare on the Day of Judgement when the first rule will be لَا ظُلْمَ الْيَوْمَ, that *no transgression will be tolerated that day.* When Allah does justice even between the animals, how can I expect that He will not take me to task on the Day of Reckoning for my own injustice."

Sufyān al-Thawrī (*Allah's mercy be upon him*) said something powerful with regards to looking at our own lives. In terms of the notion of injustice, assess, "am I actually a source of injustice in someone else's life?" Not am I being complicit in someone else's injustice? Or, am I not standing up for someone when I should be? Or, am I being fair and equitable in a situation? But am *I*, myself, guilty of harming someone or oppressing someone? Sufyān al-Thawrī said that he wished on the Day of Judgment that the only one he should have to deal with is Allah because He might forgive him for all his sins that he had committed in his relationship with Him. But Allah does not allow for a wrongdoing that we did to someone else be left unaccounted for.

Ibn Masʿūd said, "If Allah loves you then He allows all those people you wronged to be repaid from your deeds but He will increase one of your good deeds to such a size that it would cover the deficiencies found in your deeds".

We ask Allah first and foremost to protect us from being unjust to other people, to protect us from being complacent about injustice when it is apparent to us, to protect us from doing iniquitous things, and from judging in a way that's faulty when we find parties being swayed by some other interests. We ask Allah to not judge us by His justice on the Day of Judgement but to judge us by His Mercy. *Āmīn.*

11 Allah Loves
The Beneficial People

T his Hadith is often mentioned in fundraisers with regards to charity and the importance of service. But I want to really analyse this Hadith because it opens the door for other Hadith and a lot of other sayings about who Allah loves and why Allah loves those people.

We mentioned *iḥsān* earlier in the book, the concept of excellence and how Allah rewards excellence and loves it. Even though excellence is expressed primarily in the relationship between us and Allah, it's about how we treat other people in accordance to that excellence that we seek from Allah. So consider this

Hadith in light of this. The Prophet (*peace be upon him*) said أَحَبُّ النَّاسِ إِلَى اللهِ, "The most beloved people to Allah", أَنْفَعُهُمْ لِلنَّاسِ, "are those who are most beneficial to the people". It's not the best of people that are the most beneficial but the most *beloved* people to Allah are those who are the best to other people. Why? Because they amplify the attributes of Allah to other people. They serve as a vehicle of Allah's love in other people's lives and that's the best way to be earning Allah's love for yourself. The Prophet (*peace be upon him*) continued with this Hadith: إِنَّ أَحَبَّ الأَعْمَالِ عِنْدَ اللهِ, and "Verily the most beloved of actions to Allah", so now the Prophet (*peace be upon him*) is going to show us how we can be the most beneficial to the people.

Firstly, أَن تُدْخِلَ عَلَى قَلْبِ أَخِيكَ سُرُوراً that "they put a sense of inner joy into their brother's or sister's heart". They bring them inner peace. They pick them up when they're down. When they have low self-esteem, they boost them up. When they're sad or depressed or anxious, they are a source of comfort, healing and tranquillity to them. They bring them joy on the inside, they don't just smile at them; they give

56

them a reason to smile as well. They are emotionally available to people.

The way that they seek happiness from Allah, beyond all tangible things, is the same way they are most beneficial to people. They serve as a vehicle of Allah's comfort to people in the emotional sense just as they seek that from Allah for themselves.

Secondly, consider what we seek from Allah? We seek the removal of hardship. That's when people usually connect to Allah the most. But what if Allah uses us as a means of removing someone else's hardship, أَوْ تَعِنِي عَنْهُ دَيْنًا or "they remove a debt from someone", أَوْ تُطْعِمَهُ خُبْزًا, or "they feed someone a loaf of bread". You either remove a financial burden or you provide for them.

The point of this is very profound. When the Prophet (*peace be upon him*) tells us about stories of entrance to Jannah for what are seemingly small actions, they always involve service to someone else. For example, the woman who gave water to a thirsty dog; the man who removed something harmful from a path; one

Beneficial people serve as a vehicle of Allah's comfort to others in the emotional sense just as they seek that from Allah for themselves.

always finds that it is those small deeds of kindness, those small deeds of service to someone or something, or, as in the case of the man who removed a harmful thing from a path, to a whole community, by taking care of the environment. All these acts of service connect back to an outstanding reward.

Why is that? The reason is that just as we are tasked with amplifying Allah's attributes to people, if we amplify love to people, then we will receive more love from Allah. If we amplify mercy to people, we will receive more mercy from Allah. If we amplify kindness, we will receive more kindness from Allah. This is the most important point to be taken from this Hadith.

Anytime we show kindness to someone, Allah will never allow us to show more kindness to someone else than Allah will show to us. If we show gratitude to someone else, Allah will never allow us to be more thankful to someone else than He will be to us.

Our Prophet (*peace be upon him*) stated مَنْ لَا يَرْحَمْ لَا يُرْحَمْ, "Whoever doesn't show mercy will not be shown mercy", therefore whoever shows mercy will be shown mercy. ارْحَمُوا مَنْ فِي الأَرْضِ يَرْحَمْكُمْ مَنْ فِي السَّمَاء, "Show mercy to the ones on earth and the One in Heaven will show mercy to you."

The most beloved people to Allah are the ones who are most beneficial to people because Allah sees them as a vehicle, Allah uses them as a part of carrying out that relief in other people's lives. Allah will never allow us to outdo Him in these attributes, in these beautiful things that He enabled us to do in the first place.

We ask Allah to make us beloved to Him and to allow us to serve Him by serving other people and to make us the channels of *rahmah* and generosity and benevolence in people's lives and that He uses us for good all the time and not deprive us of it. *Āmīn.*

12 Allah Loves
Strength

—————— ...⟨♥⟩... ——————

We are now going to cover a set of traits that are a bit more complicated than the first set we covered. In these next few chapters, we're actually going to tackle things that people don't typically associate with righteousness and they don't associate with Allah's love.

The Prophet (*peace be upon him*) said,

الْمُؤْمِنُ الْقَوِيُّ خَيْرٌ وَأَحَبُّ إِلَى اللهِ مِنَ الْمُؤْمِنِ الضَّعِيفِ ، وَفِي كُلِّ خَيْرٌ

"The strong believer is better and more beloved to Allah than a weak believer and in all of them is good." The Prophet (*peace be upon him*) is saying that all of them are good because sometimes we do

not know where the exact *barakah* in something lies.
Someone might read this and say, "Well I'm weak
and it's not my fault and I have certain conditions or
things that hold me back."

Allah says in Surah al-Ḥadīd: وَكُلًّا وَعَدَ اللّٰهُ الْحُسْنَى,
comparing those who became Muslim earlier on to
those who became Muslim later on in the Prophet's
lifetime. Allah says: ***All of them have their allotted
promises*** but, generally speaking, a strong believer
is more beloved to Allah than a weak believer and
the Prophet (*peace be upon him*) said: احْرِصْ عَلَى مَا,
وَاسْتَعِنْ بِاللّٰهِ, "seek that which benefits you", يَنْفَعُكَ,
and "seek your strength from Allah", seek your help
from Allah وَلَا تَعْجَزْ "and don't ever be helpless and if
anything comes to you that is not to your liking then
simply say قَدَرُ اللّٰهِ وَمَا شَاءَ فَعَلَ, 'It's the decree of Allah
and what He has willed has come' and do not say 'if'
because it opens the door of the *shayāṭīn*."

The Prophet (*peace be upon him*) is talking about
strength in a very broad sense but let's focus on this
point for a moment. Islam teaches us to seek strength
in every way possible through ethical and good

The statement of the Prophet ﷺ "Don't ever be helpless" is about picking ourselves up, trying to grow, trying to be in a position of power both as an individual and as a community.

means, not through any impure things. We do not seek strength to become arrogant or proud but seek strength, in whatever capacity, so that we can actually carry out some of the things that are virtuous at a broader level and have a bigger impact. This Hadith is talking about strength of *īmān,* strength of faith, strength of resilience, strength of body and spirit, all different types of strengths. It does cover many different things and it's very clear that the Prophet (*peace be upon him*) is speaking about how our faith informs us and empowers us, so وَلَا تَعْجَزْ, "don't ever be helpless" is about picking ourselves up, trying to grow, trying to be in a position of power both as an individual and as a community. The Prophet (*peace be upon him*) said, "The upper hand is better than the lower hand", the giving hand is better than the receiving hand.

Allah says in the Qur'an as a community وَأَعِدُّوا لَهُمْ مَا اسْتَطَعْتُمْ مِنْ قُوَّةٍ , *prepare yourselves with strength,* show your strength; so we are to seek to be in a place where we can actually carry out some of those qualities. If we recall the previous chapter, we were talking about the most beloved of people to Allah and the most of beloved actions to Allah. Among them was that we have to be in a place of emotional strength to be able to help someone through their emotional vulnerability, or we have to be in a place of financial strength to be able to remove someone's debt or to be able to provide for someone who's having a difficult time providing for themselves. Some of the most beloved actions to Allah require us to be in a place of strength so that we can amplify those most beautiful attributes of Allah.

Allah doesn't want us to be weak, defeated, helpless people. In this there is a beautiful connection to *tawakkul*, to trust in Allah. Our trust in Allah shouldn't make us incapable. The Prophet (*peace be upon him*) said وَلَا تَعْجَزْ, "Don't ever be a person who is helpless", don't ever be a person who concedes, who seems to be defeated. Instead, always pick yourself up, always try to be a person who is giving rather than receiving, always seek to be someone who comforts rather than being the one comforted. That's what makes us beloved to Allah. But again وَفِي كُلٍّ خَيْرٌ, "everyone has their blessing", so don't think that if it's something outside of your circumstances that it's because Allah hates you or that you can't attain that position. This speaks to what is in our capacity, not what we are tested with.

We ask Allah to make us strong in every way possible—in our faith, in our bodies, our spirits and our minds, intellect, knowledge, our resilience, and all of the things that are implied within the Hadith and we ask Allah to allow us to use these strengths for things that are good. *Āmīn.*

13 Allah Loves

Independence

––– ···✦··· –––

In the previous chapter we talked about the strong believer. In this chapter, I want to focus on the idea of independence, which means that believers should seek to be in a position of giving rather than receiving.

The Prophet (*peace be upon him*) mentioned إِنَّ اللهَ يُحِبُّ العَبْدَ الفَقِيرَ المُتَعَفِّف, "Verily Allah loves a servant who is poor yet maintains a sense of dignity", who don't go out and beg, or put themselves in a vulnerable position but instead try to pick themselves up. The Prophet (*peace be upon him*) mentioned أَبَا العَيَالِ, even if that person has a big family, they should still do their best to be as independent as possible.

The Prophet (*peace be upon him*) taught us to seek refuge in Allah from debt, to seek refuge in Allah from being in a difficult situation, yet there are entire chapters of Hadith on the virtues of poverty. The virtues of being in tests that are not self-inflicted are that a person tries their best to maintain their modesty, and as much independence as possible, even in dire poverty. If a person finds themselves in a difficult situation and they have to resort to something they typically would not otherwise have adopted, there is a danger that this becomes a mindset, that's something the scholars have cautioned against; and a person being tested should try to avoid. Allah loves those who are trying, even in their most difficult moments, to maintain their independence as much as possible.

The Prophet (*peace be upon him*) went through numerous examples of this. ʿAwf ibn Mālik (*May Allah's mercy be upon him*) said we took a pledge (*bayʿah*) with the Prophet (*peace be upon him*) أَن لَا نَسْأَلَ النَّاسَ شَيئاً that "we would not ask people for anything" and that the Companions who were present took the pledge so seriously that if one

of them were riding an animal and they dropped
something, they wouldn't ask someone else to pick it
up for them.

A sense of independence, of self-reliance, is something
that is to be ingrained in the mindset, in the psyche.
The Prophet (*peace be upon him*) mentioned five pieces
of advice that the angel Gabriel gave him and the last
two things he said were وَاعْلَمْ أَنَّ شَرَفَ المُؤْمِنِ قِيَامه بِاللَّيلِ,
"know that the nobility of a believer is in standing
up in prayer at night", that our sense of nobility is
not with the things that other people endow us with,
it's not with the awards that are given to us, it's not
with the recognition of this world. It's in standing up
in prayer at night and it's in distinguishing ourselves
in the sight of Allah and seeking honour in His sight.
Furthermore, وَعِزَّتُهُ اِسْتِغْنَاؤُهُ عَنِ النَّاسِ, "and his sense
of dignity lies in not being in need of people", so a
person should strive as much as they can to always
be in a state of independence, whether it's financial,
emotional, physical or any other form.

Now with that being said, with all of the *du'ā's*
(supplications) that we make asking Allah to protect

us from الْعَجْزِ وَالْكَسَلِ inability and from laziness,
غَلَبَةِ الدَّيْنِ وَقَهْرِ الرِّجَالِ, from the hardship of poverty, and
from the hardship of debt. Of course, if people find
themselves in a situation where they are in need of
help, they should obviously seek help. This is speaking
to the mindset that Allah does not want us to suffer
in silence. Allah simply does not want us to resign
ourselves to a position of weakness or to a position
of being dependent. So we aim to try our best to
not adopt resignation and dependence as a mindset
and this relates back to the same strength that the
Prophet (*peace be upon him*) was speaking about as
mentioned in the previous chapter.

We ask Allah to never allow us to be in need of
anyone but Him, to make us people who always strive
for goodness and strength and make us a people
who are independent of all things but Him for surely
upon Him we are always dependent even if we don't
recognize it. *Āmīn.*

14 Allah Loves
Healthy Pride

·•·❖·•·

The word "pride" almost always has negative connotations throughout the Book of Allah and the Sunnah of the Prophet (*peace be upon him*).

The Prophet (*peace be upon him*) said that "Whoever has an atom's worth of pride (*kibr*) in his heart will not enter Jannah." It is pride that destroyed *Shayṭān*, that has destroyed many nations that came before us and many people who lived in the time the Prophet (*peace be upon him*), before him, and after him, who rejected the truth out of a sense of pride.

But what Allah does for us is that He takes qualities that could be negative and harnesses them for a greater good. As people, we naturally like to compete, so Allah didn't change the competitive nature of the *Ṣaḥābah* or the believers in general. Instead He directed their competition into something else, which was to compete for His favour. If we are competing for Allah's favour then pride does have some good connotations at times, but it's very limited and restricted to a few contexts.

We find for example that the Prophet (*peace be upon him*) talked about a person who was sitting in a gathering. Although the word "pride" was not used by him but if we consider a person of strength who sits in a gathering and people say something that is displeasing to Allah, they are speaking falsehood or backbiting and yet that person doesn't say anything. The Prophet (*peace be upon him*) said that such a person will be raised up on the Day of Judgement and asked why they did not say anything for they heard the people saying such and such. And the person will say خَشِيتُ النَّاسَ, "I was afraid of the people." The Prophet (*peace be upon him*) said that Allah will say to them that He was more worthy of being feared than those people who were around them. So, this is not pride but a sense of strength, or self-worth, to raise our voice, to speak up when something bad is happening around us.

The following Hadith is in Abū Dawūd and it has two components, we'll cover one in this chapter and the next one in the following chapter.

The Prophet (*peace be upon him*) said that there is a type of pride and the word used is *khuyalā'* not *kibr*. *Khuyalā'* is a kind of pride or boastfulness that at times is loved by Allah and at times hated by Allah; there is a type of *khuyalā'* loved by Allah and a type of *khuyalā'* hated by Allah. The Prophet (*peace be upon him*) said that Allah loves the type of pride that drives a person in battle or to give more in charity and the type of pride that Allah hates is when *khuyalā'* enables oppression. So what is the Prophet (*peace be upon him*) talking about?

In a war situation, people do war dances in advance: they boast and put on a show of strength at the start.

When I was in New Zealand, I saw the haka and I
thought it was the most beautiful thing I'd ever seen
in my life, I want my kids to be able to do that, to
make a show of strength. The Prophet (*peace be
upon him*) lived amongst a people who were very
proud of their ability to fight on the battlefield, which
benefitted Islam and the believers. Proud warriors had
entered Islam and that meant something when they
were going to battle against a much bigger army.

There's a narration about the famous warrior Abū
Dujānah who had a certain swagger. He had war
dances and a red bandana he would tie around his
head before battle. The Prophet (*peace be upon him*)
saw Abū Dujānah's swagger and said that this is a
walk that is hated by Allah, except before a battle. So
this type of pride before battle is a good thing because
the benefit of instilling confidence in allies and fear in
enemies outweighs the typical harms of such an act.

When it comes to charity, a competitive person
is driven to compete for the favour of Allah.
Competitiveness in charity is bad if a person boasts
to make others feel guilty or has other bad intentions

e.g. if they want to be seen as more generous than others or if it becomes a matter of ego. Tribalism is a horrible thing but the Prophet (*peace be upon him*) allowed tribes to encourage one another to compete in trying to do good. That is the way Abū Bakr and 'Umar competed with one another in doing good. In other words, we should aim to move forward, to serve, to give more in charity and compete in goodness, this sense of taking pride to gain the favour of Allah, is good. It is driven by a good intention and a good purpose and the result of it is goodness as well.

Allah dislikes the type of pride where one starts to harm someone else, where one starts to become arrogant, where one loses sight of the goal and acts in a way that is disliked by Allah. So once again, this speaks to the qualities of strength that Allah loves, when a person feels motivated and competes for the goodness of pleasing Allah and takes pride in always trying to do the best of deeds with the best of intentions. We ask Allah to grant us this type of healthy pride in doing good and always having a sincere motive. *Āmīn.*

We should aim to move forward, to serve, to give more in charity and compete in goodness, this sense of taking pride to gain the favour of Allah, is good.

15 Allah Loves

Honour

— ···❦··· —

Once again, we're taking a quality that usually has negative connotations but, in this situation, it has some good implications. Before I get back to the Hadith that we started in the last chapter, I want to mention another Hadith about envy (*ḥasad*) because it is tied to jealousy, although it's not exactly the same thing.

The Prophet (*peace be upon him*) mentioned that there is no envy except in two situations: when you envy someone who Allah has given knowledge to and they spread it or because Allah has given them wealth and they spent it in His cause. Why? Because

that envy would not be of the kind that we want
something for ourselves, in other words, the money
for the sake of being rich or knowledge for the sake
of being praised. The envy would be at the good that
they are able to do with what Allah has given them;
we don't wish bad for them but we wish that we too
could also do the good that they are doing and do it
for a noble goal. With a noble intention; we are not
envious over this worldly life (*dunyā*), nor envious in
the way *Shayṭān* is, nor having an evil intention nor
wishing another ill, and this speaks to our priority of
seeking the Hereafter.

The word "jealousy" is a little controversial, because
there is really no direct translation for *ghīrah* in the
English language that really fits. We could translate
it as "honour" or as "a sense of protective jealousy".
In the same Hadith in Abū Dawūd, that I mentioned
in the previous chapter, the Prophet (*peace be upon
him*) mentioned that there is, غِيرَةٌ يُحِبُّهَا اللهُ, a type of
ghīrah that Allah loves and a type of *ghīrah* that He
hates. Allah loves protective honour and jealousy that
is based upon solid grounds; the type that He hates is
all based on suspicion.

I want to focus on the term *ghīrah* and see how it can be important for us. When we see someone being harmed, our brother or sister or even a stranger being harmed, being taken advantage of, how do we respond? There's a clip of Malcolm X, El-Hajj Malik El-Shabazz, speaking about the black women in America, and how she's the most disrespected person in America. We can see the outrage that he has, his protective nature, how he would not let anyone disrespect black women in America. Now, I want us to think about how we feel about our sisters being offended, being taken advantage of, being assaulted anywhere in the world. If that doesn't drive a sense of outrage and honour in us, then that is a problem.

If we see our brothers and sisters from the Rohingya who are being racially discriminated against or the Uyghurs or wherever it may be. We see brothers and sisters who did nothing but live their lives in a noble way and didn't seek to harm anyone but because they are Muslim, they are being harmed, they are being abused, their dignity is being taken away from them. This should drive a sense of honour that disturbs us, disrupts us and makes us want to do something to help them.

We are moved by something when we have *ghīrah* for religious symbols, for Allah and for his Messenger. I am not referring to when people disrespected the Prophet (*peace be upon him*) and that caused Muslims to take to the streets and break windows and burn tyres and harm people. That is not because of love for the Prophet (*peace be upon him*) but because of a cultural sense of disrespect and a very false sense of honour. But we should be driven to do something—we should feel disturbed on the inside—but we want to uphold the image of the Prophet (*peace be upon him*) in a noble way that befits his nobility. Likewise, a person should feel that *ghīrah* for their family, a sense of protectiveness, of honour. A woman should be protective of her husband and a husband should be protective of his wife in a way that they wouldn't like either person to be abused or harmed.

Someone might say that this is the language of honour killings. Absolutely not! Honour killings are among the most hated of things in Islam. They are not an honour for Allah, they are the greatest violation of Allah that a person hurts an innocent

Allah encourages believers to act honourably and protect and uphold the honour of our fellow brothers and sisters.

girl or an innocent woman or even a woman or a girl who has done something wrong in such an atrocious manner. This is not from the Sunnah and it is not from Islam. Honour killings have nothing to do with Islam and they are motivated by something other than Allah and other than the Messenger (*peace be upon him*).

Allah encourages us to act honourably and protect and uphold the honour of our fellow brothers and sisters. We should not be suspicious, become abusive or harmful to others or be driven to lowly acts. Instead, we should uphold the nobility of noble things and that means the sanctity of what Allah has sanctified, including the honour of people and the dignity that Allah has bestowed upon human beings, especially those who are beloved to us. Allah loves healthy pride and protective jealousy, having a great sense of honour, tied to honouring the dignity of others.

We ask Allah to give us those things without letting them become a means of transgression and to keep within us only that which is positive. *Āmīn.*

16 Allah Loves

Gentleness

-...-

In the last chapter we talked about honour and having a sense of protection. Prior to that we discussed strength, now we are going to discuss it from a different angle. We are going to show how the concept of gentleness is not contradictory to what we have discussed earlier.

The Prophet (*peace be upon him*) was walking with ʿĀʾishah (*Allah's mercy be upon her*) in Madinah and there was a group from the People of the Book that yelled out سَامٌ عَلَيْكُم which means "May death be upon you". The Prophet (*peace be upon him*) said وَعَلَيْكُم, "And upon you", keeping himself composed

and calm. ʿĀʾishah (*Allah's mercy be upon her*) was
outraged by the fact that they spoke to the Prophet
(*peace be upon him*) that way and she yelled back at
them وَعَلَيكُمُ السَّامُ وَاللَّعَنَة, "And upon you is the curse
and the anger [of Allah]", she started to shout back
at them but the Prophet (*peace be upon him*) asked
her to calm down. She said "Don't you know what
they said? Didn't you hear what they said to you,
O Messenger of Allah?" He replied, "Didn't you
hear what I replied?" and then he said to ʿĀʾishah
(*Allah's mercy be upon her*) very beautifully that
إِنَّ اللهَ رَفِيقٌ يُحِبُّ الرِّفْقَ فِي الأَمرِ كُلِّه, "Allah is gentle and He
loves gentleness in all things."

When we read the *Sīrah* of the Prophet (*peace be upon
him*), do we read it to confirm an attribute that we
already have? If a person wants to be strong or wants
to justify their behaviour in a certain context, do they
go and take an incident from the Prophet's life (*peace
be upon him*) where he demonstrated a sense of anger,
or a sense of aggressiveness, that wasn't commonly
in his nature? Or even the opposite position where if
a person wants to justify any type of engagement or
compromise they normally use the Treaty (*ṣulḥ*) of

Ḥudaybiyah as an example to justify their position and
so on. But to read the *Sīrah* honestly and truthfully,
the default of the Prophet (*peace be upon him*) was
that Allah loves gentleness in all affairs. If the Prophet
(*peace be upon him*) departed from gentleness it
was for a good reason. It was to send a very specific
message in a very specific context.

So what does that mean and how do we understand
gentleness. Just as Allah is gentle, Allah is kind; Allah
also has attributes that denote punishment, that
denote a sense of anger. A changed context doesn't
mean Allah stops being *al-Raḥmān, al-Raḥīm*
and *al-Wadūd* or *al-Ghafūr*. Rather it means there
are contexts that determine that type of response.
However, the general default teaching of the Prophet
(*peace be upon him*) is gentleness in all of our affairs.
By understanding the Sunnah in a holistic way we
learn to appreciate that we don't have to be loud,
aggressive or foul to denote strength, rather those
things are actually a sign of weakness.

The Prophet's composure in the face of the taunts and
insults he received in Makkah and Madinah were

signs of strength, that he wasn't going to allow his enemies to get into his head or drive him away from his principles, from his ethics. The Prophet (*peace be upon him*) speaking in a calm manner, not raising his voice at people to win an argument, not cutting people off and not demonstrating aggression even when he (*peace be upon him*) was at the height of his power, was a symbol of strength. Consider that Allah, despite having complete authority over His entire creation choses to show us gentleness and kindness.

We too, show our greatest strength when we are in positions of power but we too opt for gentleness and kindness, not in a way that would cause injustice to become rampant but in a way that would stop us from becoming unjust ourselves or departing from our natural core of goodness. So إِنَّ اللهَ رَفِيقٌ يُحِبُّ الرِّفْقَ فِي الأَمْرِ كُلِّه, "Allah is gentle and He loves gentleness in all things."

We ask Allah to place gentleness within us and to allow us to act upon it even when the Devil tries to stoke our anger and cause us to depart from it. *Āmīn.*

17 Allah Loves

Humility Without Disgrace

---- ···❖··· ----

We have covered healthy pride, honour and other things that typically don't get associated with positive connotations in the Qur'an and the Sunnah of the Prophet (*peace be upon him*) and then we discussed gentleness in the previous chapter. Now the best way to merge these concepts together is to look at this beautiful *āyah* in the Qur'an in which Allah talks about the group of people He loves. Allah says to the believers:

مَن يَرْتَدَّ مِنكُمْ عَن دِينِهِ فَسَوْفَ يَأْتِي اللهُ بِقَوْمٍ يُحِبُّهُمْ وَيُحِبُّونَهُ أَذِلَّةٍ عَلَى الْمُؤْمِنِينَ أَعِزَّةٍ عَلَى الْكَافِرِينَ يُجَاهِدُونَ فِي سَبِيلِ اللهِ وَلَا يَخَافُونَ لَوْمَةَ لَائِمٍ

That *whoever amongst you turns away from his religion then Allah will replace them with people who love Allah and are beloved to Him.* Allah mentions that these people truly love Allah and they are truly loved by Him. Then Allah refers to their characteristics and says they are humble amongst the believers and that they carry themselves with dignity amongst the disbelievers and they don't fear the blame of the blamers. We discussed earlier about healthy pride and unhealthy pride, but there's also unhealthy humility or disgrace. Imam al-Ghazālī has an entire chapter distinguishing a positive sense of humility from an unhealthy humility that leads to disgrace. So, أَذِلَّةٍ عَلَى الْمُؤْمِنِينَ أَعِزَّةٍ عَلَى الْكَافِرِينَ, being humble amongst the believers and being dignified amongst the disbelievers. Does this mean being disrespectful to those who don't believe? Does this mean harming them? No, we just covered in the previous chapter the Prophet (*peace be upon him*) maintaining a sense of collectedness and composure in the face of taunts and insults. What is meant by dignity among the disbelievers is that we don't relinquish our faith or our principles or our Islam in the presence of other people who do not share our faith.

Let's compare these two qualities together and think about how we apply them today, أَذِلَّةٍ عَلَى الْمُؤْمِنِينَ, *humble amongst the believers*. Today we find people who carry themselves with such courtesy and dignity amongst people who aren't Muslim but when they are amongst their own they become ruthless. One of my teachers talked about خُذُوا زِينَتَكُمْ عِنْدَ كُلِّ مَسْجِدٍ, that you take your beauty to the *masājid*. This doesn't mean your beautiful clothes but your beautiful character (*adab*). There are people who might be so courteous at work, but when they come to the *masjid* then suddenly out of a sense of overfamiliarity they demonstrate a certain sense of pride and arrogance amongst the believers. This is not the way we are called to be. أَذِلَّةٍ عَلَى الْمُؤْمِنِينَ, Allah says we should humble ourselves with extra humility amongst the believers and that humility is actually a very strong word "ذِلَّة", which means "humiliation", that you bring yourself down, lower your wing, and always deal with the believers with a great sense of humility.

This does not mean that we do not deal with humility with people who aren't believers, but it cannot be that that humility leads us to disgrace ourselves amongst people without *īmān*. For instance, they might go out into public and will not only accept taunts or indignities from people but they'll actually hide their faith. They may even relinquish it.

Somebody might look at this verse and assume it gives them licence to go to their non-Muslim neighbours, bang on their door at Christmas and tell them to take down their decorations? No. What it does mean is that on Eid we go over with a sense of pride, tell them how as Muslims we have just fasted the month of Ramadan. And that we would like to share this celebration with them and share gifts with them. This is the opposite of relinquishing our faith in the presence of the people who don't believe in it. Allah says that يُجَاهِدُونَ فِى سَبِيلِ اللهِ, *they strive in the path of Allah,* وَلَا يَخَافُونَ لَوْمَةَ لَائِمٍ, *and they don't fear the blame of the blamers.*

Ibn al-Qayyim (*Allah's mercy be upon him*) draws our attention to the fact that Allah did not say, the blame of disbelievers, because often the people who persecute us the most or try to shame us out of our Islam, are other Muslims.

There are certain Islamic acts that we do that our non-Muslim friends accommodate and accept but when we are amongst Muslim relatives they want us to stop doing them. They feel ashamed of them and have internalized that humiliation (*dhillah*) from the outside world to the point that they are now most vicious with people on the inside and it speaks to a collective issue. So لَوْمَةَ لَائِمٍ *they don't fear the blame of the blamers:* no one can push us away from our faith from either inside or outside the community. No one can shake us out of our own ethical core, out of our own principles of good character (*adab*) or virtue (*akhlāq*) from inside or outside. No one can force us to act rudely or to relinquish anything of what Allah loves from inside or outside. This is a package that comes together.

Imam Ḥasan al-Baṣrī (*Allah's mercy be upon him*) is very insightful on this issue. He said that the curse of the believer is that he excels in one good quality and so he tolerates the bad quality that comes with it. We mentioned healthy pride earlier, but it's very rare to find people that can utilize good pride when it's necessary and good humility when it's necessary. It's very hard to find people that can strike that balance.

We ask Allah to give that balance to us and make us humble in His sight and proud of the things that He teaches us to be proud of and be beloved in His sight as a result of that. *Āmīn.*

18 Allah Loves

Forbearance and Deliberation

···❖···

There is a special story that I learned very early on while I was studying the lives of the Companions of the Prophet (*peace be upon them*). A lot of the time when we hear Hadith about rushing to do good, there is a danger that it could lead a person to not be very deliberate in their actions.

This Hadith relates to a long incident, the backdrop is of multiple tribes coming to meet the Prophet (*peace be upon him*). People were rushing to get off their camels and horses, and run to the Prophet (*peace be upon him*) so that they could greet him and could kiss his hand. There was however one person who stayed back for some time. That person was al-Ashaj ʿAbd al Qays. Al-Ashaj was a young Anṣārī who was very deliberate and calculated about the things that he did. He made sure everything was in order and stayed behind to make sure that his tribe had all of their belongings with them, tethered the camels and horses properly, and then he went and changed and made himself presentable before he went and exchanged *salām* with the Prophet (*peace be upon him*). Some of his tribe mocked his deliberation or thought he was being slow but the Prophet (*peace be upon him*) said to him that إِنَّ فِيكَ خَصْلَتَيْنِ يُحِبُّهُمَا اللهُ "You have two qualities that Allah loves about you." And he said, "What are they, O Messenger of Allah?" and he replied الْحِلْمُ، وَالأَنَاةُ, "Your forbearance and deliberation."

Forbearance and deliberation are tough words, so let me explain them. Forbearance is when you are particularly patient with people, it's about patience and holding yourself back. It is relatively easier to be patient with a natural disaster, with something bad happening that is outside of anyone's control rather than with someone in front of us who is really testing our patience.

So, the incident we covered a few chapters ago
with 'Ā'ishah (*Allah's mercy be upon her*) and the
people that shouted out سَامٌ عَلَيْكُم, "Death to
you", to the Prophet (*peace be upon him*) who
showed forbearance. He was holding himself back
and restraining himself. If we have forbearance
(*ḥilm*) we are able to exercise self-control. That is
why Ibrahim (*peace be upon him*) is described as
ḥalīm, and one of the names of Allah is *al-Ḥalīm,*
One Who is forbearing. Allah is forbearing with
us, Allah tolerates our weaknesses, our wickedness,
and Allah does not punish us right away but instead
He gives us a chance. So *ḥilm* is shown when a
person is forbearing, they are calculated, they are
well restrained, and their anger is only for specific
contexts and is carried out in a way that is pleasing
to Allah; *al-anāh* is the related quality of being
calculated, of being deliberate, of making sure that
you do things properly.

الْأَنَاةُ *al-anāh* is the opposite of haste. The Prophet
(*peace be upon him*) said that الْعَجَلَةُ مِنَ الشَّيْطَانِ
"Haste is from the Devil." But *al-anāh* (deliberation)
is from Allah. *Al-anāh* is when a person takes their

Allah is forbearing
with us, Allah tolerates
our weaknesses,
our wickedness,
and Allah does not
punish us right away
but instead He gives
us a chance.

time to make sure that everything is done right, that nothing is out of order, and just as they have a great sense of self-control, they have great control of their environment as well. They are making sure that they are always doing things properly, calculated, in a structured way, in a way that sustains progress rather than hinders it. Not in a way that would make progress too slow but in a way that would maintain a steady momentum towards Allah, towards these good things.

So *ḥilm* and *al-anāh* come from the same well, which is to be forbearing, to be calm, to be collected, to be deliberate about what we do. It is Allah Who has this quality Himself. He loves to see us be forbearing, to take our time and make sure that things are done right, that we don't rush, that we are not hasty with the things that we do. Some people might criticize this as being slow but it is not slow; in the same way that some people might criticize a person who doesn't react to insult or to foulness in a like manner as being too slow or reserved. But these qualities are beloved to Allah because they are done from a place of intentionality and we as believers are taught to be intentional about the things that we do, so we seek to manifest forbearance and deliberation in our personality, in our work and in how we control the environment. *Āmīn*.

⑲ Allah Loves
Due Diligence

━━━━━━━━━━━ ⋯⋯❖⋯⋯ ━━━━━━━━━━━

The next quality is one that builds upon the last two qualities and is manifested in our methodology and our work ethic. The Prophet (*peace be upon him*) said that إِنَّ اللهَ تَعَالَى يُحِبُّ إِذَا عَمِلَ أَحَدُكُمْ عَمَلاً أَنْ يُتْقِنَهُ, "Allah loves that when any one of you undertakes a task, they do it right." In other words, they do it with due diligence, that they give it their fullest attention.

اتقَان (*itqān*) means excellent work ethic or due diligence; اِحْسَان (*ihsān*), which I mentioned earlier, is excellence but in the broader sense of always trying to set higher standards for ourselves. *Iḥsān* refers to motivation, to the drive that we have with regards to Allah; *itqān* refers to the higher work ethic. So, not just a higher standard in motivation alone but a higher standard in work ethic also and this is testimony to a higher standard of motivation as well.

If we have *itqān,* due diligence in our work ethic and are detail-oriented, that speaks to a superior degree of motivation as well, to a greater level of *iḥsān.* If we look at Islamic history and see the way that we produced incredible architecture, calligraphy, and all of these things where great attention to detail was invested, these were people who paid close attention to everything they did and so it carried over into a superior work ethic as well, which in turn led to such advancement. I want us to really pay attention to this with regards to the work that we do, particularly when it's Islamic work, when it's any work of service.

Too often we excuse bad work in the name of it being a good cause. I'm volunteering, I'm doing this for the sake of Allah so it's okay if it's sloppy. I don't have to pay attention. It's not like I'm getting paid for this; it's not like I'm at work and I've got a boss to worry about. But wait! Who is paying us for Islamic work?

And who are we doing it for? It's someone greater than our boss and greater than any money we might get. We do things with a superior work ethic because we have a superior motivation. Allah loves to see that in the work that we do, whether it is secular or religious, that we pay attention to the details, that we have a higher standard that we place on ourselves. *Iḥsān* is usually spoken about in the capacity of worship, so when we are worshipping Allah, for Allah's sake, then it had better be distinguished worship.

Likewise, if we are working for Allah then it had better be distinguished with regards to our work ethic as well. Paying attention to the details, making sure that we are doing things right, bringing the spirit of *iḥsān*, and the work ethic of *itqān*, together. To aim to merge these two forms of excellence: a higher standard in motivation combined with a higher standard in the work we do as well.

We ask Allah to grant these two things to us so that it shows both in our drive and the result of our drive, that it shows both in our work and in our worship.

101

We ask Allah to make us beloved to Him and to allow this to be a testimony for us on the day of Judgement. *Āmīn.*

20 Allah Loves
Consistency

···❦···

We are often reminded of this Hadith especially as we get to the end of Ramadan. We are encouraged to make sure that we continue the deeds that we learnt and practised in Ramadan. But the reality is that all of us experience a drop-off after Ramadan.

In this Hadith the Prophet (*peace be upon him*) was asked أَيُّ الأَعْمَالِ أَحَبُّ إِلَى اللهِ "Which actions are most beloved to Allah?" and he answered, أَدْوَمُهَا وَإِنْ قَلَّ "Consistent ones, even when they are small." So, the most beloved of good deeds to Allah are the consistent ones even if they are small.

'Ā'ishah (*Allah's mercy be upon her*) said in the family of Muhammad (*peace be upon him*) إِذَا عَمِلُوا عَمَلًا أَثْبَتُوهُ, "When they did a good deed, they maintained it." A person might wonder, "How am I going to continue *tarāwīḥ* after Ramadan?" Well, *tarāwīḥ* is just *qiyām al-layl* (the night vigil) but there is no way that we are going to be able to pray the same amount after Ramadan. There is no way that we are going to fast every day after Ramadan. There is no way we are going to be able to maintain the same level of remembrance (*dhikr*) or charity. But maintaining consistency is a sign of our love for Allah and is a sign that we are loved by Him.

How does consistency speak to the love of Allah in particular? The scholars explained it in this way: they said, if a person is able to maintain consistency in doing a good deed, that's actually a testimony of it being sincerely for Allah. Why? Because if one wavers in doing good deeds then it's probably a sign that there are external circumstances that drive the performance or lack of performance of those good deeds. This means that these good deeds rest upon something other than the love of Allah or at least are highly motivated by things external to the love of Allah. If a person is able to be consistent with a good deed, even if it's small, then that's a sign they are also consistent in their love of Allah, that they are maintaining the steady presence of Allah's love and of concern for Allah's love in their lives no matter what is happening to them, no matter what their emotional state is, no matter what's taking place.

When it comes to the last ten nights of Ramadan, we are supposed to push ourselves to the greatest levels of worship and then suddenly we hit this wall of Eid where we stop doing everything altogether. What does this say about our consistency with Allah?

We should aim to think of the things that we will be able to continue with outside of Ramadan and let them be small, reasonable goals. We should not be guilted into thinking that if we do something small after Ramadan then it is a sign that our Ramadan has been lost. Take small things on so we can continue doing those good deeds, *inshā'Allāh,* so that when the time comes again when good deeds are increased and amplified, we will be able to kick into the next gear without it seeming foreign to us. If we pray *qiyām* throughout the year then when *tarāwīḥ* comes we have amplified the *qiyām* and taken it to the next level.

The Prophet (*peace be upon him*) said "Do the deeds that you are able to continue with. Take up things that do not exhaust you. Allah does not tire of your worship until you tire of worshiping Allah. The most beloved of deeds to Allah are the small ones, if they are consistent." May Allah allow us to take some of the good deeds that we perform in Ramadan and to maintain them throughout the year, and throughout our lives, until we meet Him. *Āmīn.*

21 Allah Loves
Punctual
Prayers

We talked earlier about consistency, about the methodology of being consistent as being the most beloved quality of good deeds. Our aim should therefore be to apply this to the most beloved of good deeds. We know the Prophet (*peace be upon him*) said that the very first thing that we will be asked about on the Day of Judgement is the prayer (*al-ṣalāh*).

As he was passing away, the Prophet (*peace be upon him*) said, الصَّلَاةَ، الصَّلَاةَ، وَاستوصُوا بِالنِّسَاءِ خَيْراً, "Your prayer, your prayer and treat your women well."

Prayer is the most fundamental pillar of Islam after a person enters into the fold of Islam with the testimony of faith. The Prophet (*peace be upon him*) taught us to practice this fundamental pillar with consistency. The Hadith that we are going to cover in this chapter is from 'Abdullāh ibn Mas'ūd (*may Allah be pleased with him*) who said "I asked the Prophet (*peace be upon him*): أَيُّ العَمَلِ أَحَبُّ إِلَى اللهِ, 'Which actions are most beloved to Allah?' The Prophet (*peace be upon him*) responded, اَلصَّلَاةُ لِوَقْتِهَا, 'Prayer on time.'" In another narration the Prophet (*peace be upon him*) said, اَلصَّلَاةُ لِأَوَّلِ وَقْتِهَا, "A prayer at the beginning of its time."

It sounds simple but let's consider this for a moment. A lot of times when we are talking about *qiyām al-layl* (the night vigil), the *tarāwīḥ* prayer, the Sunnah prayers and those extra deeds we can do, we forget about the five obligatory prayers.

The first thing we will be asked about are our obligations, the most important part of our religion, the first of which are the five daily prayers. Praying them on time, guarding them, making sure that we are following all the pillars of the prayer itself, and making sure we are not omitting anything. That is the most beloved thing we can do for Allah.

Even though we should be talking about the night prayer and the Sunnah prayers because they serve as a cover for the obligatory prayers but realize that the obligatory prayers are at the core of it all. That is why the Prophet (*peace be upon him*) said, "On the Day of Judgement if they have deficiencies in their obligatory prayers, Allah asks, 'Where are the voluntary prayers?'" and Allah starts to fill the missed obligatory prayers or the deficiencies in the obligatory prayers with them. The voluntary prayers are meant to cover for the deficiencies we have in the obligatory prayers: we obviously have stray thoughts that take us away from the prayer, disturbances and other distractions.

Let's focus on prayer at the beginning of its time for a moment. What makes it so beloved to Allah? Indeed, this is the case for all prayers except for the 'Ishā' prayer, in which there is a preference for delaying it a little bit. What makes the beginning time of prayer so special? It shows Allah that when we hear

حَيَّ عَلَى الصَّلاةِ، حَيَّ عَلَى الفَلَاح, "Come to prayer, come to success" that we are eager and longing for Him as we come to prayer. Ibn al-Qayyim (*Allah's mercy be upon him*) said, "Come to Allah—بِقَلبٍ مُشتَاق—with a heart that is longing for Him", with a heart that is in anticipation of Him. The Prophet (*peace be upon him*) used to say أَرِحنَا بِهَا يَا بِلَال, "Comfort us with prayer, O Bilāl!" He also used to say that prayer was the coolness of his eyes. Prioritizing prayer in our lives shows that we are prioritizing Allah in our lives.

Allah fully understands there are other things that get in the way, in terms of career, school, travel and other things that will cause us to have to push prayer to a later moment within its set time. Of course, when we are travelling, we may combine prayers. But in our normal day, in our normal routine, how early do we perform the prayer once its time has started? We will notice that at the end of the day it is the same five prayers that we are going to pray; it is just a mindset that we have to decide upon. Some people wait until five minutes before the next prayer, others do it within five minutes of the time beginning. It is the same five prayers that both sets are praying but it

The Prophet ﷺ
used to say that
prayer was the
coolness of his eyes.
Prioritizing prayer
in our lives shows
that we are
prioritizing Allah
in our lives.

is the mindset, the attitude that they have with Allah. And Allah says in the Qur'an about the hypocrites: وَإِذَا قَامُوا إِلَى الصَّلَاةِ قَامُوا كُسَالَى, *When they get up for their prayers, they get up lazily.* They don't feel like doing it. They are dragging their feet: they barely catch the prayer. Allah also tells us about the nations that came before, فَخَلَفَ مِن بَعْدِهِمْ خَلْفٌ أَضَاعُوا الصَّلَاةَ that *there came after them generations who lost their prayer,* وَاتَّبَعُوا الشَّهَوَاتِ *and followed their desires.* Due to this, they would find punishment.

'Umar ibn al-Khaṭṭāb (*may Allah be pleased with him*) commented on this saying, أَضَاعُوا الصَّلَاةَ *they lost their prayers* means that they started to delay the prayers beyond its permissible time. They would pray 'Aṣr at the time of Maghrib instead. If we delay our prayers habitually, then eventually we are going to start praying them late and then we are going to start missing prayers altogether. It's a natural regression that takes place. And then they followed their desires.

In the *āyah* that came before that verse, Allah mentions in Surah Maryam that there was a group of righteous people who, when they heard the verses of

al-Raḥmān (the Most Merciful), خَرُّوا سُجَّدًا وَبُكِيًّا,
they fell down on their faces, prostrating and crying.
ʿUmar had a beautiful way of explaining this verse,
he said that in the verse when Allah mentions the
righteous, they had *Khuḍūʿ* خُضُوع which is to humble
yourself in a bodily fashion, namely, to stand before
Allah in the proper way, to guard the physical elements
of the prayer. So, they fell on their faces in prostration
before Allah and they also had *Khushūʿ* خُشُوع or
humility, which is the internal discipline that caused
them to cry. Their next generation lost both their
physical and their internal discipline. Outwardly
they lost their prayers, while inwardly they longed
for other than Allah.

Ibn al-Qayyim (*may Allah have mercy upon him*)
wrote a very powerful point on this idea of prayer.
He said that, إِذَا دَخَلَ عَبْدُ اللهِ الصَّلَوةَ, "When a servant of
Allah enters into the prayer, ثُمَّ الْتَفَتَ, then he turns
away from Allah." This is not a physical turning
away from Allah but an internal turning away from
Him. قَالَ اللهُ عَزَّوَجَلَّ Allah Glorified and Exalted says
to the servant, يَا عَبْدُ إِلَى أَيْنَ خَيْراً مِنِّي, "O my servant,
where are you turning to that is better than Me?"

Have you found something better than Me? More worthy than Me?

So, let's start with the basics. If we can get anything right, let us try to make your five daily prayers on time and make it a habit to start praying early in the allotted time so that we don't start missing the prayers. This would be a blessed task with Allah. The Prophet (*peace be upon him*) said "When a person comes on the Day of Judgement having prayed their five prayers on time, not omitting anything out of them, understanding their importance then they have Allah's promise that He will enter them into Paradise".

We ask Allah to make us punctual in our prayers, to enter us into Paradise and to forgive us for our shortcomings and to make us amongst those who long for Him. *Āmīn.*

22 Allah Loves

Cleanliness

In the last chapter we covered consistency in praying on time. What precedes the prayer is *wuḍū'*, our purification ritual. *Wuḍū'* comes out of a larger concept of cleanliness, of purity, طَهَارَة.

The Prophet (*peace be upon him*) said that cleanliness (*ṭahārah*) is half of faith and a lot of people who came out of the Sunday Islamic School system or went to the *masjid* to learn or had aunties and uncles who constantly told them that you have to be clean and you've got to do this a certain way and do that a certain way, never fully grasped the love of Allah that is embedded in the concept of purifying oneself.

Allah tells us in the Qur'an about the people who
are established within the *masjid*, that,
فِيهِ رِجَالٌ يُحِبُّونَ أَنْ يَتَطَهَّرُوا وَاللهُ يُحِبُّ الْمُطَّهِّرِينَ, *in it are*
men and women who love to purify themselves and
Allah loves those who are pure. This type of purity is
obviously referring to again the physical and spiritual
but it's a greater level of purity than simply doing
wuḍū', than simply washing oneself.

The Prophet (*peace be upon him*) taught us to
take care of removing impurities from ourselves
and making sure that our *wuḍū'* is done carefully
not quickly, that we do our *wuḍū'* with proper
supplications, that we freshen our breath before we
come to the *masjid*. The Prophet (*peace be upon
him*) used to purify his mouth with the toothbrush
(*miswāk*) every single time he would pray. Yet he
didn't place any hardship on the ummah by requiring
all of us to do that. However, this was done in
preparation for meeting with Allah in the prayer.
Prayer on time shows prioritizing Allah in terms of
our schedule and thus the way we pray shows us
prioritizing Allah over our thoughts and distractions.
The scholars have mentioned that the way that we

purify and prepare ourselves for these meetings really speaks volumes about the longing we have for Allah.

Imam al-Ghazālī (*Allah's mercy be upon him*) said that when anybody goes to meet their most beloved one they make sure they are properly dressed, washed, they spray on their best cologne or perfume, comb their hair, comb their beards or whatever it is that they do to prepare themselves in the most beautiful of ways. So how is it that we purify ourselves when we go to meet the Most Loving (*al-Wadūd*), the One that loves those that purify themselves? The care with which we prepare ourselves shows our anticipation therefore taking due care of our *wuḍū'* is a means of taking care of our prayer, as well as of showing Allah the great desire we have to meet with Him.

These are the things to take into consideration when we beautify ourselves but to begin with let's start with the importance of removing offensive things prior to prayer. The Prophet (*peace be upon him*) told us not to come to the *masjid* with garlic breath or after having eaten onions because that's offensive to the angels, as well as offensive to the people standing next to us. Taking care of those things is a means of generosity (*ikrām*) to those that are around us as well as to the angels, whom we can't see, but most of all a means of demonstrating the anticipation we have of standing before Allah.

The Prophet (*peace be upon him*) taught us very profoundly to use a minimal amount of water while making *wuḍū'*, whereas we splash ourselves with as much water as possible. When he (*peace be upon him*) made *wuḍū'*, he used very little water. It was the attention he paid, making sure that the water covered his fingers properly, getting into all the places it needed to, when washing the feet by going between the toes with a wet finger. These things may seem minimal, but they express something greater: a greater attention and a greater appreciation. As was mentioned before, we should have *itqān,* or attention to detail in the way that we purify ourselves prior to worship.

We ask Allah to make us amongst those who are spiritually purified and physically purified when we go to meet Him for the sake of spiritual purification. *Āmīn.*

23 Allah Loves
The Mosque

————— ◈ —————

We've covered prayer and purification. Now we're going to cover the *masjid*. I know that we have heard many Hadith about the importance of the *masjid* but let's cover them again within this context.

The Prophet (*peace be upon him*) said that, أَحَبُّ الْبِلَادِ إِلَى اللهِ مَسَاجِدُهَا, "The most beloved of places to Allah are the mosques, and the most hated of places to Allah are the marketplaces." We often talk about *masjids* and their central importance in our lives and what this means in terms of the love of Allah. Obviously, it is the house of Allah and he who makes seeking Allah his primary concern then everything that's beloved to Allah becomes beloved to him. The house of Allah becomes his own house and that is why the Prophet (*peace be upon him*) said that, الْمَسْجِدُ بَيْتُ كُلِّ مُؤْمِنٍ, "The mosque is the home of every single believer."

The Prophet (*peace be upon him*) forbade those who tried to forbid their wives from going to the *masjid* and he used a powerful rhetoric to do so, لَا تَمْنَعُوا إِماءَ اللهِ مَسَاجِدَ اللهِ, "Don't forbid the female servants of Allah from the houses of Allah" because these houses of Allah are meant to be their homes as well. Every single believer, even a child, is meant to regard the house of Allah as the primary home in their own lives; the place that they go to for mercy, tranquillity, and for nourishment and there is absolutely no replacing the role of a *masjid* in one's life with anything else. There are other places where believers could get together and do *ḥalaqahs* or gatherings. There are other places that they could get together to socialize, and they can pray in other places too. We can form a congregation in our own home but there's no place like the *masjid*. Why is this the case?

The *masjid* is a place for prostration (*sujūd*), the place of the remembrance of Allah, which is why it is the most beloved place of Allah. How many people remember Allah in the marketplaces? Think about *dhikr* versus lack of *dhikr,* the remembrance of Allah versus the lack of remembrance of Him? At the time of the Prophet (*peace be upon him*) there was no concept of night clubs or bars or things of that sort so let's just confine ourselves to the two most functional places in a person's life, the marketplace and the *masjid*. In the marketplaces it's very hard to remember Allah and that is why there is such reward for making the relevant supplications upon entering the marketplace,

لَا إِلَهَ إِلَّا اللهُ وَحْدَهُ لَا شَرِيكَ لَهُ، لَهُ الْمُلْكُ وَلَهُ الْحَمْدُ، يُحْيِي وَيُمِيتُ وَهُوَ حَيٌّ لَا يَمُوتُ، وَهُوَ عَلَى كُلِّ شَيْءٍ قَدِيرٌ

"There is no God but Allah, He is One and there is no partner with Him, He is ever-living and never dies, He gives life and He causes to die and He has dominion over all things."

The Prophet (*peace be upon him*) mentioned the great reward of saying this particular supplication upon entering the marketplace because it isn't

easy to remember Allah in the marketplace. In the
masjid, we are surrounded by the remembrance
of Allah or we should be. The Prophet (*peace
be upon him*) also extended the idea of places in
which Allah is remembered versus the places in
which Allah is not remembered to every other
social gathering and things we do in our lives. He
said the most blessed gatherings are the ones in
which Allah's name is mentioned and the worst
ones are the ones in which His name is never
even mentioned. So, to remember Allah in our
gatherings, in our spaces beyond the *masjid* is
certainly beloved. But this Hadith has a greater
dimension, especially in the twenty-first century,
where the *masājid* are not just a place for *dhikr*.

Imam al-Nawawī (*may Allah have mercy upon
him*) commented on this Hadith and said one of
the reasons why the *masjid* is beloved to Allah is
because of the type of interaction it fosters between
the people who go there. It's a place where we come
to seek mercy but it is also supposed to be a place
of exchanging mercy. In the marketplace we usually
see division or argument. There's deception, there is

haggling, there are false oaths and all types of things. Imam al-Nawawī said the *masjid* is ideally supposed to be a place where none of that is present. It's supposed to be a unifying place where there is mercy, tranquillity, harmony and nourishment; instead of false oaths there is calling upon Allah, in place of deception there is truth and admission.

It's not just the space of the *masjid* versus the space of marketplace because certainly the Prophet (*peace be upon him*) taught us how to engage in both spaces, ethically. Rather, it's how we turn the *masjid* into the most beloved place to the Prophet (*peace be upon him*), to Muslims, to Allah. How do we take this *masjid* and turn it into the Madanī (Madinan) community that the Prophet (*peace be upon him*) established, where we're not just remembering Allah in the *masjid* but cultivating through that *dhikr* a certain type of interaction between each other in the *masājid* such that the same spirit is carried into the marketplace.

We should also acknowledge that the Prophet (*peace be upon him*) said, "The *masjid* isn't a place for buying and selling." He also said that "If you see people doing trade within the *masjid* tell them, 'May your transaction not be blessed.'" So, the *masjid* is supposed to be a place reserved for Allah's remembrance. May Allah fill our lives with its mercy and tranquillity and make it of central importance to us and dedicate us to making the *masjid* the closest to the *masjid* of the Prophet (*peace be upon him*) so that it could be the most beloved to him. *Āmīn.*

24 Allah Loves

Love

---- ···◈··· ----

In this chapter we will look at a very particular kind of love; love for Allah's sake. This is something that is specific and special about our religion. Allah talks about the wonder of it, just looking at the earliest generation of Muslims, Allah says,

وَاعْتَصِمُوا بِحَبْلِ اللهِ جَمِيعًا وَلَا تَفَرَّقُوا وَاذْكُرُوا نِعْمَتَ اللهِ عَلَيْكُمْ إِذْ كُنْتُمْ أَعْدَاءً فَأَلَّفَ بَيْنَ قُلُوبِكُمْ فَأَصْبَحْتُم بِنِعْمَتِهِ إِخْوَانًا

Hold firmly to the rope of Allah and do not be divided. Remember Allah's favour upon you when you were enemies, then He connected your hearts, so you, by His grace, became brothers.

It wasn't just a superficial connection or one that
was forced by the Prophet (*peace be upon him*) to
bring people together. ***Your hearts became connected
to each other,*** which is the requirement for other
types of unity to be able to take hold,
فَأَلَّفَ بَيْنَ قُلُوبِكُمْ فَأَصْبَحْتُم بِنِعْمَتِهِ إِخْوَانًا, *so you became*
brothers, for otherwise you would have wanted to
kill each other but Allah saved you from yourselves.
That is what is so special about this love; this
brotherhood in Islam unifies people across race,
class, social barriers, preferences and hobbies. It
brought those people together, who would have been
unlikely to have any friendship outside of something
as powerful as Islam, and they loved each other for
Allah's sake. But what does it mean to love each
other for Allah?

The Prophet (*peace be upon him*) mentioned those
that are shaded by the throne of Allah. The Prophet
(*peace be upon him*) informed us that one of those
categories is the person who is tied to the mosque.
And the very next category is two people who love
each other for Allah and for absolutely nothing else.
Allah binds them, they come together for Allah's love,

and they part from one another for Allah's love The Prophet (*peace be upon him*) said in a very beautiful narration in *Ṣaḥīḥ Muslim* that there was a man who was walking to visit his brother in another town and an angel came to him in human form and asked, "Why are you going to visit so-and-so?" He replied, "By Allah, the only reason that brought me out to visit him is because I love him for the sake of Allah." And the angel replied, "Then know that I am a messenger of Allah sent to tell you that Allah loves you because you love Him." When we love for Allah's sake, then know that Allah loves us. The Prophet (*peace be upon him*) said "Allah has said that on the Day of Judgement, 'Those who love each other for My sake are under My shade and under My glory.'" In this world too, the love we have for Allah's sake is an unbreakable bond. It's also a form of cover, shade and glory in this world that brings people together in a really transformative way: it extends communities of love, in which people love each other for the sake of Allah.

The Prophet (*peace be upon him*) also said that if we love someone for the sake of Allah, then we should

The Prophet ﷺ said, "When two people mutually love each other for Allah's sake, the one who is stronger in loving will be more beloved by Allah."

tell that person that we love them for His sake. This can get awkward sometimes because saying "I love you" is something we might say to a spouse, a son or a daughter, but how many times do we tell a fellow brother or a fellow sister that we love them for Allah's sake? We can tell our spouses too, but expressing that love for Allah's sake is an important part of it. As the Prophet (*peace be upon him*) said "When two people mutually love each other for Allah's sake, the one who is stronger in loving will be more beloved by Allah." It's not just about two people loving each other for Allah, but how much we love the other person for Allah's sake is proportionate to how much Allah loves us for that love.

The Prophet (*peace be upon him*) told us in a beautiful Hadith that "When Allah loves someone, he calls Jibril, his beloved one, and says, يَا جِبْرِيلُ ، إِنِّي أُحِبُّ فُلَانًا فَأَحِبَّهُ 'O Jibril! I love this person so you should love this person too,' so Jibril loves that person. Then Jibril calls the angels and says 'Allah loves that person so you should love that person too,' so all the angels love that person too. And then the inhabitants of heaven love that person because Allah loves that person, and then

يُوضَعُ لَهُ القَبُولُ فِي الأَرْضِ acceptance and love is put in the hearts of the people on this earth." This final part means that the people love something of you that's true about you and Allah causes them to love what made you beloved to Him in the first place. So, it's the type of people who Allah directs toward you, who love you and what they love you for is in fact true of you.

We ask Allah to make us amongst those who love and are loved for His sake and who are all brought together by loving Him and being loved by Him and that are shaded by His glory on the Day of Judgement because of His love for us and our love for Him. *Āmīn*.

25 Allah Loves
Your Mother

In the last chapter, we discussed loving someone for Allah's sake and unfortunately, a lot of times, we immediately extend this to mean people outside of our household. However, we forget the people inside our own homes, and there is no person we should think of more when we hear this Hadith, than our mother. A man asked the Prophet (*peace be upon him*), "To whom should I give my honour and my kindness?" The Prophet (*peace be upon him*) said, "Your mother." And then he enquired, "Then who?" and the Prophet (*peace be upon him*) replied, "Your mother." And then he enquired again, "Then who?" and the Prophet (*peace be upon him*) replied again,

"Your mother." Then he asked yet again, "Then who?" and the Prophet replied, "Your father."

So, we know that Allah has preferred the mother in a very special way. The Prophet (*peace be upon him*) sent a Companion back to his mother saying, "Paradise lies at the feet of your mother." Allah has mentioned obedience to parents with obedience to Him in the Qur'an, that we worship and obey Him, and that we show a similar level of kindness and love to our parents without of course worshiping them or preferring them over the Creator. The point is that Allah mentioned obedience to them alongside obedience to Him. وَقَضَىٰ رَبُّكَ أَلَّا تَعْبُدُوا إِلَّا إِيَّاهُ وَبِالْوَالِدَيْنِ إِحْسَانًا He included them by saying: *Your Lord has judged that you worship no one but Him and that you show only excellence to your parents.* I have to give a qualifier here that this does not mean tolerating injustice, harm or oppression from our parents as part of our love for them. These are circumstances outside the scope of the default position and need to be dealt with as exceptional cases. In general, however, the high status of the mother and this concept of earning the love of Allah by showing love to our mother is the default position.

Even if we have committed a major sin, between us and Allah, we should go ahead and show goodness to our mother and see if it is a way of opening that door of pleasure with Allah.

There are two narrations I want to share with you. One of them is from the Prophet (*peace be upon him*) and the other one is from ʿAbdullāh ibn ʿAbbās (*may Allah be pleased with him*), the Prophet's cousin. A man approached the Prophet (*peace be upon him*) and said to him, "I have committed a major sin. Is there a way for me to repent to Allah?" The Prophet (*peace be upon him*) asked, "Is your mother alive?" He said, "No." Now look at the follow-up question of the Prophet (*peace be upon him*). He asked, "Does your mother have a sister who is living?" The man said, "Yes." The Prophet (*peace be upon him*) said then go and be good to her, show her some excellence and hope for Allah's mercy in the process. So, after the mother, the Prophet (*peace be upon him*) immediately asked if he had a maternal aunt (*khālah*). Of course, in those societies and in many societies today, the maternal aunt plays a motherly role in a person's life and the Prophet (*peace be upon him*) mentioned that, اَلْخَالَةُ بِمَنْزِلَةِ الأُمِّ, "She has the station of the mother." She is second when it comes to honour and love. So even if we have committed a major sin, between us and Allah, we should go ahead and show goodness to our mother and see if it is a way of opening that door of pleasure with Allah.

The narration from Ibn ʿAbbās (*Allah's mercy be upon him*) is a very profound one. A man came to Ibn ʿAbbās and confessed to him that he had killed someone because he had become jealous of them and asked if he had any hope of Allah's forgiveness. Ibn ʿAbbās replied, "Is your mother alive?" Ibn ʿAbbas was worried about the man's Hereafter (*ākhirah*) hence this was separate to any legal proceedings or form of retribution that may have been the case. The man said, "No." Ibn ʿAbbās responded, "Well, just go and seek Allah's forgiveness sincerely and hope in His mercy".
He gave him a generic answer after asking him specifically if his mother was alive. The students of Ibn ʿAbbās, the scholars of this ummah, asked him why he had asked the man about his mother as she was not really a part of the equation for his major sin. The man had killed somebody, and was worried about forgiveness from Allah, and whether he still has a chance of Allah's mercy, yet why did you (Ibn ʿAbbās) ask about his mother? Ibn ʿAbbās replied, "By Allah, I don't know any action more beloved to Allah than serving your mother."

Showing kindness and obedience to one's mother is one of those things that is so easy for us to do and so accessible for us. If our mothers are still alive, we should make sure we do what is right. Furthermore, Zayn al-ʿĀbidīn said, "If one gate is closed, then go to another". So, to please our father, to show our love for our father and to obey him is a route to Allah's love and mercy too. The Prophet (*peace be upon him*) also taught us that "The pleasure of your father is the pleasure of Allah," so our parents are truly gates of Paradise. Serving them, showing kindness to them, showing love to them, especially as they become older. Show patience with them as they get older. There are no two people whom we can love for Allah's sake more than our parents.

We ask Allah to be pleased with us and to join all our parents, spouses, children, brothers, sisters, aunts, uncles together for the sake of Allah's love, and we ask Allah to grant us the highest level of *Jannat al-Firdaws*. *Āmīn*.

26 Allah Loves

The Unnoticed

---...❖...---

This one is a little complicated. Allah loves those who are unnoticed; Allah loves those who are obscure, Allah loves those who are hidden; Allah loves those people who are barely noticeable in gatherings. Who are these people? You may remember a Hadith related by Sa'd ibn Abī Waqqās (*Allah's mercy be upon him*), إِنَّ اللهَ يُحِبُّ الْعَبْدَ التَّقِيَّ الْغَنِيَّ الْخَفِيَّ, "Truly Allah loves those servants who are pious, self-sufficient, and obscure", who are unnoticed by the people, who avoid the spotlight, avoid any prominence. There are different ways of being noticed. It's one thing to be noticed because of good deeds, but it's obviously showing off (*riyā'*) if we seek to be noticed because of our good deeds. If someone is doing goods, then obviously there is a noticeable amount of it that will be public at times. In this situation, however, it is a different type of obscurity that the Prophet (*peace be upon him*) is praising.

The Prophet (*peace be upon him*) was once sitting with his Companions and a man walked by and the Prophet (*peace be upon him*) asked, "What do you think of this man?" They responded, "O Messenger of Allah, he is the most prominent of people. If he intercedes on someone's behalf, then his intercessions will be accepted. If he proposes to someone then his proposal will be accepted." That man walked away and the Prophet (*peace be upon him*) saw another man and asked, "What do you think of this person?" and they said, "O Messenger of Allah, this man is poor. If he intercedes on someone's behalf then his intercessions won't be accepted and if he proposes then his proposal will surely be rejected." Then the Prophet (*peace be upon him*) said, "But one of this person is better than an earth full of the other person, in the sight of Allah."

Here is where this Hadith becomes fascinating—
some of the most beloved people to Allah are among
the least noticed in our communities. The friends
(*awliyā'*) of Allah, those closest to Him are the hidden
gems (*akhfiyā'*) in our communities. It is a person
who is quiet, does their service, does their worship,
always greets people with a smile, who is barely
noticed in gatherings, doesn't boast and, in fact, they
are gaining a special type of prominence in the sight
of Allah. The Prophet (*peace be upon him*) taught us
that it's a good habit for us to have obscurity and it's
part of modesty (*ḥaya'*). He (*peace be upon him*) said
that the best person is the one who sits in gatherings
and when he leaves people barely notice him.

The kind of gathering being talked about here is
not one of *dhikr* or remembrance of Allah, but one
where there may be some idle speech or discussions
that are not very beneficial. In those gatherings these
people maintain a low profile, remain quiet and have
a sense of humility. That shows us that such people
are engaged in something else. They are engaged in
another type of pursuit. They are not seeking their
value through how other people see them.

This is not about being noticed for good deeds, or competing for good deeds that Allah talks about in the Qur'an, or about the presence of virtue in public which must be done only for His sake. This is a person who keeps quiet, maintains softness, humility, and modesty in gatherings and amongst the people and does not show off, does not speak too much, does not talk out of turn, does not place too much importance on themselves or in their own voices.

If we connect this to the very first Hadith that was listed above, if a person is wealthy, that would give them some sort of prominence. If a person is famous that might give them some sense of self-importance, as a result they do not know how to sit in gatherings and not be rich and famous anymore. And that is actually a very big problem.

The Prophet (*peace be upon him*) was the most famous person in this world, but at the end of his life when he walked into a gathering you could not distinguish him. The Prophet (*peace be upon him*) observed long periods of silence. The Prophet (*peace be upon him*) did not take the fame provided to him by Allah for being his Messenger and project that on to all of his affairs. Likewise, ʿUthmān (*Allah's mercy be upon him*) was one of the richest Companions of the Prophet (*peace be upon him*) but he would be the least noticeable Companion if he walked into a gathering, such was his humility.

I have to end with this because I find it so profound. When the Prophet (*peace be upon him*) woke up one day and he noticed that the woman who used to clean the *masjid* was not there, the Companions said, "O Messenger of Allah, she passed away and we didn't want to wake you up at night, so we buried her because we didn't want to bother you." This meant they thought she was an insignificant person in the community, just a woman who cleaned the *masjid*. The Prophet (*peace be upon him*) was so upset by this and said, "Take me to her grave." Then he prayed on her again as if the *janāzah* of the Companions wasn't enough. He prayed on her again and said that his *ṣalāh* is a means of light for the person in the grave.

There is a great lesson in this for us. Although this woman was unnoticed by the people, Allah noticed her.

May Allah notice us, may Allah allow us to seek recognition from Him and learn to practice humility, obscurity, modesty, silence, not to let people carry our stuff, not to look at us in a certain way or to talk to us in a certain way. We should try our best to always maintain a sense of modesty and to seek the love of Allah even when we are surrounded by other than Allah. May Allah make us amongst them. *Āmīn*.

27 Allah Loves

Generosity
→ *in Trade* ←

⸻ ···❦··· ⸻

In this chapter we look at a common scenario that takes place when we are negotiating or making a trade. For those who don't live in the Middle East, if you go to *ʿumrah* or *ḥajj* or to certain countries where there aren't fixed prices for things then you have to negotiate in a marketplace. Allah has given us our sustenance (*rizq*) and our circumstances. For some people an extra dollar doesn't mean that much, but for others it could make or break the transaction.

The Prophet (*peace be upon him*) says in this Hadith, إِنَّ اللهَ يُحِبُّ سَمْحَ الْبَيْعِ سَمْحَ الشِّرَاءِ سَمْحَ الْقَضَاءِ, "Allah loves the one who is generous when he buys, generous when he sells, and generous in repayment." Of course, this means being easy-going in collecting repayment, in no way does it include any type of interest or usury (*riba*) at all.

One of the first groups of people Allah warned about in the Qur'an was وَيْلٌ لِلْمُطَفِّفِينَ, *those who cheat with scales* and this means any tiny additions to get a little something extra out of the transaction. The believer is more worried about being charged by Allah because they have wronged a person in business than making a little something extra. The Prophet (*peace be upon him*) mentioned that Allah is pleased with honest merchants and salesmen, with someone who's an honest trader, who doesn't cheat people or take anything extra. They seek extra from Allah and the Prophet (*peace be upon him*) instead, whether they are buying, selling, dealing with debt or repayments. There are various narrations on how we deal with one another in trade.

None of this, however, implies being a fool when we buy or sell. This doesn't mean being taken advantage of, but rather not being someone who goes overboard with haggling. It means not being someone who cheats, but being someone who is considerate, someone who does not sacrifice or compromise any of their principles in the process of trying to get a few extra *dirhams, dīnārs,* or dollars in the process of buying or selling something in an unprincipled way. It's okay to make some money but sometimes we also have to have a generous heart. If Allah has enabled us and it is easy for us to walk into a marketplace and buy things, then we don't really have to worry about the extra dirham or dollar. On the other hand, it might make a huge difference to that salesperson if they get the extra five riyals, dirhams or dollars. Let them have it, as that person may indeed be in need and that is part of excellence (*iḥsān*)—if you are generous to someone who is trying to make an honest living but are having a hard time.

In some countries, we see people trying to sell tissue boxes or trying to sell other small items. It does not hurt us, *inshā'Allāh*, to buy from them as a means of *ṣadaqah*, just for the sake of honouring a person who is trying to get by through making an honest living. Always remember that Allah loves a person who is considerate in the process of buying, selling and repayment.

We ask Allah to make us amongst them. *Āmīn.*

28 Allah Loves

Those Who Follow the Prophet ﷺ

⬧⬥❦⬥⬧

The qualities that have been discussed in this book are embodied most in the personality of the Prophet Muhammad (*peace be upon him*) and therefore I want to share a relevant *āyah*. When Allah tells us in the Qur'an,

قُلْ إِنْ كُنْتُمْ تُحِبُّونَ اللهَ فَاتَّبِعُونِي يُحْبِبْكُمُ اللهُ وَيَغْفِرْ لَكُمْ ذُنُوبَكُمْ وَاللهُ غَفُورٌ رَحِيمٌ

Say: if you truly love Allah then follow me and Allah will love you back and He will forgive you for your sins and Allah is the most Forgiving and the most Merciful, when we read that *āyah* do we think to ourselves, how can I be like the Prophet (*peace be upon him*)?

The Prophet (*peace be upon him*) had such a comprehensive character, وَإِنَّكَ لَعَلَىٰ خُلُقٍ عَظِيمٍ, *Truly, you have an exalted standard of character,* that Allah had praised, that He had crafted and He gifted the Prophet (*peace be upon him*) with the best of manners. The Prophet (*peace be upon him*) gives us something to aspire to in every single aspect and element of our lives.

However, I want to go into another dimension of this. The Prophet (*peace be upon him*) mentioned the great reward of reviving a Sunnah, a prophetic tradition. We often find that a lot of these good qualities are things we see in people or in isolated incidents but they are not necessarily tracing them back to the Prophet (*peace be upon him*) or even tracing them to any type of religious grounding. But when we start to practice one of the good qualities we have been discussing in this book and we trace it back to the life of the Prophet (*peace be upon him*); we revive a Sunnah, a tradition of the Prophet (*peace be upon him*) in our lives and this is the greatest way to earn the love of Allah.

Yet we may ask ourselves: can we actually be like the Prophet (*peace be upon him*)? We may think that no matter what effort we put towards worship; we are never going to be able to worship Allah the way he used to worship Allah. No matter how much we try to practise mercy, kindness, generosity, diligence or any of those different qualities that we have covered in this book, we are never going to have enough of that quality. We are never going to have what the Prophet (*peace be upon him*) had and that is why it is so important to note that this verse ends so beautifully by saying that by our trying to be like the Prophet (*peace be upon him*) Allah will overlook our shortcomings and Allah is (*al-Ghafūr*) the One Who Covers and Forgives faults and Who Shows a Special Mercy (*al-Raḥīm*) because we are trying.

It is an acknowledgement from Allah that even if we are never going to get there, it is the fact of trying sincerely that He loves, as we discussed in an earlier chapter. We look at the life of the Prophet (*peace be upon him*) and try to bring his qualities into our life. Although reviving a Sunnah in smaller matters is good too as it could carry a major reward and we do not belittle any actions that we do for Allah, no matter how tiny they are. However, to think about those bigger qualities that we have looked at in this book and know that even if we cannot be just like the Prophet (*peace be upon him*), the fact that he becomes the standard that we are seeking, is enough for Allah to love us. يُحْبِبْكُمُ اللّٰهُ وَيَغْفِرْ لَكُمْ ذُنُوبَكُمْ, *He loves you back, and overlooks any of your shortcomings.*

We ask Allah to make us like the Prophet Muhammad (*peace be upon him*), to make us love him and to join with him under his love in *Jannat al-Firdaws*. *Āmīn.*

29 Allah Loves

Acceptance
⟿ *of His Gifts* ⟾

---···◈···---

We have mentioned qualities we try to attain that are human manifestations, human vehicles of the things that Allah has prescribed for Himself. In these situations, we must recognize we have a Lord who is Loving, Merciful, and Generous. He does not want to torture His servants. We take this very powerful understanding of Allah from the Prophet (*peace be upon him*) who said that, إِنَّ اللهَ يُحِبُّ أَن تُؤْتَى رُخَصَه, "Allah loves that you accept His concessions."

Another narration of Imam Aḥmad (*Allah's mercy be upon him*) adds that "the same way He loves that you avoid the things that are acts of disobedience to

Him. Allah loves that you accept His gifts, that you take the easy way He has given you, that you take His concessions."

Another narration says that, "the way that He loves that you take the harder things, the more difficult things that have an inherent level of struggle and burden in them, He also loves you to take advantage of the things that He's made easy for you." So, for example, in Ramadan, Allah doesn't want us to torture ourselves. If a person is travelling and it is difficult to fast while travelling, they do not have to fast that day, as Allah does not want us to harm ourselves. Allah has given a gift to a traveller and Allah loves that a person takes advantage of that and accepts the gift. The Prophet (*peace be upon him*) saw two groups of Companions and he said, "The reward belongs to those who broke their fast and travelled, because they took the gift of Allah." If people are travelling, do they shorten their prayer (*qaṣr*) or do they perform the full prayers? It is more rewardable to shorten the prayers, when we travel, as we are following the Sunnah of the Prophet (*peace be upon him*) in accepting a concession and a gift from Allah.

We have a Lord Who loves to be generous. Remember that we pray in the last ten nights of Ramadan, "O Allah! You are Forgiving and Generous. You love to forgive, so forgive us."

When we break our fast, remember that the Prophet (*peace be upon him*) told us, أَحَبُّ عِبَادِي إِلَيَّ أَعْجَلُهُمْ فِطْرًا, "The most beloved of my servants to me are those who break their fast quickly." Allah does not want us to delay breaking our fast after the time of Maghrib has arrived. It should not be that we prolong breaking the fast and lengthen the time before we quench our thirst or hunger. When the time for Maghrib starts, Allah wants us to go ahead and eat our date and drink our glass of water.

At the same time, Allah wants us to delay our *suḥūr* until the time of Fajr, just before the time that it is no longer acceptable because it shows we are taking advantage of the gifts that Allah has given to us. We have a Lord Who loves to be generous. Remember that we pray in the last ten nights of Ramadan, اَللَّهُمَّ إِنَّكَ عَفُوٌّ كَرِيمٌ تُحِبُّ الْعَفْوَ، فَاعْفُ عَنَّا, "O Allah! You are Forgiving and Generous. You love to forgive, so forgive us."

The Prophet (*peace be upon him*) tied that to Allah's generosity too, for just as Allah loves to forgive us, loves to be generous with us, He loves that we accept

His gifts when He gives them to us. That does not however mean, taking the concession (*rukhṣah*) in a legal opinion (*fatwa*) by "taking the easiest fatwa all the time". It means that when there is something that is of ease embedded within the Sharia, within *fiqh*, within an act of worship, we should take that and thank Allah for it. That is an expression of gratitude to Allah in itself and Allah loves to pardon, He loves to forgive, He loves to make things easy for us.

He says in the Quran that, يُرِيدُ اللّهُ أَن يُخَفِّفَ عَنكُمْ, *Allah wants to lighten the burden upon you, and that,* يُرِيدُ اللّهُ بِكُمُ الْيُسْرَ وَلاَ يُرِيدُ بِكُمُ الْعُسْرَ, *Allah desires ease for you not hardship.* This *āyah* from Surah al-Baqarah comes in the context of Allah making concessions for a sick person, and for a traveller, to not fast. We should not harm ourselves and say that it is for Allah, use the concession, the gift, that Allah has given to us. Thank Allah for it and that is the most rewarding thing that we can do; with the Lord Who loves to forgive, loves to be Generous and loves for us to accept His gifts.

May Allah make us amongst the people who attain His forgiveness, and who receive His gifts in this life and in the Hereafter. *Āmīn.*

30 Allah Loves
Beauty

············⟨❦⟩············

llah loves beauty, for, إِنَّ اللهَ جَمِيلٌ يُحِبُّ الْجَمَالَ, "Allah is beautiful and He loves beauty." This Hadith speaks to the etiquette and a general mindset that we are supposed to have, although it is especially relevant on the Day of Eid. The Prophet (*peace be upon him*) said, "Whoever has in their heart an atom's weight of pride will not enter Paradise." And one of the Companions asked, "O Messenger of Allah, [but] a person loves to have nice clothes, and they love to have nice shoes?" The Prophet (*peace be upon him*) replied, "That's praiseworthy", إِنَّ اللهَ جَمِيلٌ يُحِبُّ الْجَمَالَ, "Allah is beautiful, and He loves beauty."

The Prophet (*peace be upon him*) also said, "If Allah has given you a blessing, Allah loves to see its effect upon you, so enjoy the blessing but don't be extravagant." So, to dress nicely, to put on our best clothes, to take the blessings that Allah has given us and to show it but not to show it off. Instead, show our blessings with gratitude. Let the trace of Allah's blessings be seen upon us, taking care of ourselves, being well dressed, showing that blessing, and thanking Allah for it. Allah also says in the Qur'an: خُذُوا زِينَتَكُمْ عِندَ كُلِّ مَسْجِدٍ, *Take your best appearance when you go to Allah's house.*

And there is no greater demonstration of that than on Eid day when the Prophet (*peace be upon him*) told us to come out in our best form, to wear our best clothes, to show the best of adornment, within what is permissible, and to thank Allah.

After the long month of Ramadan, we thank Allah and we come out with our best on Eid day, showing that beauty for the sake of Allah who is the Most Beautiful, within permissible boundaries. We should adopt that mindset for our entire lives: Allah does

158

not want us to look beaten down and showing that
we are poor or deprived when Allah has given to us.
He wants us to show our best as a means of showing
our gratitude for His blessings. That is why Imam
al-Ghazālī (*Allah's mercy be upon him*) mentioned
people who would wear wool even when they didn't
need to, or wore certain clothes that were beat-up or
raggedy, that they deprived themselves because they
thought it was an expression of love for Allah. But
we have a Lord Who is generous and wants to see the
trace of His blessing upon us, so enjoy His blessings.

ʿUmar ibn ʿAbd al-ʿAzīz (*Allah's mercy be upon him*)
advised us, "Speak of your blessings without boasting,
without showing off and without attracting envy."
When people talk about attracting envy, most of the
time, the people who are very paranoid about envy
are the people who want to show off the most, who
have the most extravagant weddings and the most
extravagant things. Instead we must do things in a
moderate way without being extravagant and say,
اَلْحَمْدُ لِلّٰهِ, all the time. We let the gratitude show in the
actions with the beauty that Allah has given to us.

We ask Allah to always envelop us in His Beauty, embrace us in His Beauty, and embrace us in His Love.

O Allah, Most Generous and Most Forgiving, I pray that You accept this book, and pray that it benefits its readers as a road-map on how to become most beloved to You and in ways that are most pleasing to You. *Āmīn.*